THE DIARY OF JOHN STURROCK

SOURCES IN LOCAL HISTORY NO 4

The *Sources in Local History* series is
sponsored by the *European Ethnological
Research Centre* c/o the National Museums
of Scotland, Queen Street, Edinburgh
EH2 1JD

General Editor: Alexander Fenton

THE DIARY OF JOHN STURROCK, MILLWRIGHT, DUNDEE 1864–65

Edited by

CHRISTOPHER A. WHATLEY

TUCKWELL PRESS
In association with the
University of Dundee Archives
and Manuscripts Department

In memory of Joan Auld (1938–1995)

First published in Great Britain in 1996 by
Tuckwell Press
The Mill House
Phantassie
East Linton
East Lothian EH40 3DG
Scotland

Introduction copyright © Christopher A. Whatley, 1996

ISBN 1 898410 72 0

British Library Cataloguing in Publication Data

A catalogue record for this book is available
on request from the British Library

Typeset by Hewer Text Composition Services, Edinburgh
Printed and bound by
Cromwell Press, Melksham, Wiltshire

LIST OF CONTENTS

ACKNOWLEDGEMENTS

Richard Cullen of Dundee Archive and Record Centre generously and for no reward applied his genealogical skills on my behalf to find the dates and places of John Sturrock's birth and marriage. He is a credit to his profession. Professor G. I. T. Machin, until recently Head of the Department of Modern History, University of Dundee, kindly read and commented upon the text of the Introduction. Any remaining flaws of course are my own responsibility.

Several years ago, a former colleague, Dr Annette M. Smith, drew my attention to the diary and accounts. Had she not done so, they might still be lying, forgotten or little-used, on a shelf in the University Archives. That they have finally been published is in no small part due to the warm reception I had when I showed them to John and Val Tuckwell, of Tuckwell Press, and Professor Sandy Fenton, of the European Ethnological Research Centre.

My father, H. A. Whatley, generously undertook the laborious task of preparing the Index. He also drew my attention to otherwise unnoticed typographical errors.

My greatest debt however is to my dear friend and long-time historian colleague Dr Michael J. Bartholomew, of the Open University. As Summer School tutors on the Open University's Arts Foundation Courses since the late 1970s, we have both made use of pages of Sturrock's diary and accounts as instances of primary sources which provide a unique and telling route into the lifestyle and mind of a respectable mid-Victorian artisan. It was Dr Bartholomew's continued enthusiasm for the material and continuing discovery of new possibilities within the evidence which largely convinced me that John Sturrock's papers should be published. The way that literally hundreds of students, including members of Dundee University's Modern History Department's 'Victorian City' class, have responded to and learned from them left me in no doubt.

Finally, I should acknowledge the assistance provided by Mrs Joan Auld, formerly Archivist at the University of Dundee who tragically died in a mountaineering accident in September 1995. Joan Auld was the inspiration and driving force for the Archives and Manuscripts Department at the University. John Sturrock's diary is just one part of a massive collection of historical records pertaining to Dundee and its region which she gathered over a period of just under twenty years. It is a collection which is of local, national and international significance. Featuring business records but also containing rich seams of material for social historians as well as other sub-disciplines within history, Joan Auld's work will be of inestimable benefit to many generations of historians. Joan was desperately excited by this and other publications which made use of materials in her care. She located the cover illustration for this book. She will be sorely missed.

CAW

DUNDEE UNIVERSITY LIBRARY DEPARTMENT OF ARCHIVES AND MANUSCRIPTS

The University of Dundee Archives and Manuscripts Department holds and manages a large manuscript collection including a substantial collection of business records, mainly relating to the jute industry in Dundee and India. Other aspects of the manuscript collection include records relating to medicine, religion, shipping and railways. A growing element of the collection relates to environmental history, including manuscript and photographic records.

The Archives also hold the records of the University of Dundee and its predecessors, University College, Dundee and Queen's College, Dundee; the Brechin Diocesan Library manuscripts and other church records; and the Tayside Health Board Archive. Non-manuscript materials include a map and plan collection and an extensive photographic collection. The Archives also manage the Kinnear Collection, a large collection of books and pamphlets of local interest and the Joan Auld Memorial Collection, consisting of books and pamphlets on the theme of labour history.

Summary lists of the collection are available from the Archives and source lists are available on various subjects including Accident registers, Agriculture, Children, Pre-1850 material, Genealogy, First World War, Literature, Medicine, Science and Technology, Second World War, Shipping, Transport, Women and Working Conditions and Health.

The Archives are situated in the Tower Building basement of the University. For further information contact: The University Archivist, Tower Building, The University, Dundee DD1 4HN or see the Archives world wide web site at: http:www.dundee.ac.uk/Archives/

INTRODUCTION

It was not common for working men in Britain in the nineteenth century to keep daily diaries.[1] The survival of the diary of John Sturrock, a Dundee millwright in the early mid-Victorian era, is therefore significant, especially as accompanying it are a set of the author's immaculately detailed income and expenditure accounts.[2] It is much to be regretted that his 'work book', which recorded the various jobs he did, and the overtime he worked, appears to have been lost. The diary however does include some information about his hours and the nature of his employment.

What first-hand knowledge we have of the doings, lifestyles and attitudes of the working classes has largely been derived from autobiographies. Scotsmen (rather than Scotswomen) produced a disproportionate number of these.[3] It is well to note however that one of the most frequently quoted of them, James Myles' *Chapters in the Life of of A Dundee Factory Boy*, first published in 1850, is decidedly not the autobiographical account its title suggests. Rather, it is a didactic novel, written by a former Chartist, a self-made and self-educated man with a moral mission. Myles never worked in a mill or factory.[4]

It is Sturrock's diary however which is the subject of this volume. Although the diary and accounts only cover a short period of time (fifteen months in the former case, a year in the second), they provide a unique record of John Sturrock's habits and interests at this time in his life, when he was in his mid-20s. Later in this 'Introduction', attention will be drawn to some of the more noteworthy of these.

Sturrock of course was one man, and as has been indicated, the very fact that he kept a diary makes him unusual. Even rarer is the regularity with which he kept it. What will be seen to be his voracious reading of particular types of books and magazines tends to stand him apart too: David Vincent, the modern master of the working class autobiography, has observed that the pursuit of knowledge 'was and has remained a minority tradition within the working class'.[5] Yet this does not detract from the value of the source. It is vivid in its detail, and provides a remarkably rich insight into Sturrock's character. Readers will gather from this, and from his habits and pastimes, that he can be firmly located within the 'respectable' working class in Victorian Britain. It is this which gives the source its widest interest. The steadiness of Sturrock's life which the diary conveys, bears witness to its realism; most lives were and are like that. Sturrock however is not simply a cipher; he is complex and even contradictory. There was also an unmistakably Scottish dimension to him. In addition, the diary reveals much about Dundee in this crucial period in the town's development, or at least those aspects of it which were of interest to Sturrock. These offer a new and refreshing insight into Victorian Dundee, which sometimes contrasts sharply with the received view.

Images of Dundee in the mid-nineteenth century are almost uniformly dismal. These are not without foundation. Later than Glasgow or Paisley, Dundee's textile industry had taken off in the 1820s; during the following two decades, as with much of the rest of urban industrial Scotland, the town had experienced the shock of industrial revolution, at the core of which were three major waves of mill and factory building, a vast expansion in shipping activity, and a doubling (between 1821 and 1841) of the town's population, to 63,000.[6] In the early 1800s descriptions of Dundee were of a modest-sized, comfortable and relatively peaceful Scottish town. By 1837 a permanent military presence had been established in Dundee, while in 1842, such was the apprehension of a Chartist-led armed rising that some 500 special constables were sworn in and ready to defend the mills against attack.[7] At the turn of the 1840s the Rev George Lewis, minister of St David's parish, reported that on a recent visit to England he had 'looked in vain for the evidence of deeper physical degradation' than that which confronted him every day in Dundee.[8] He was convinced that parts of Dundee (and Glasgow) were worse than anything he had seen in the English manufacturing towns of Bolton and Manchester. Certainly within the context of Scottish urban society in the nineteenth century Lewis's impressions find statistical support. Although much smaller in size than Glasgow, throughout the century Dundee and its west coast counterpart were unenviably yoked with similar statistics of social suffering. Death rates and

levels of overcrowding and drunkenness were worse than the
other larger Scottish towns, while Dundee's record on infant
mortality was the poorest of all.[9]

As is well known, the fortunes of its inhabitants were more
than usually dependent upon a single volatile industry, coarse
textiles, and in this sense Dundee stands apart from the other
main Scottish cities.[10] Compounding the problem was the
fact that profit margins on most heavy linens and jute were
slim (fortunes were made by buying raw materials cheaply,
and by volume production), international competition was
increasingly severe after the mid-1850s, and wages were
amongst the lowest in the British textile industry.[11] These
were paid to an overwhelmingly female labour force, although
not insignificant numbers of young males were also employed,
until the age at which they would have to be paid adult rates,
when they were turned out (around 800 per annum in the later
nineteenth century), unless they were destined for careers as
overseers or mechanics, or the few other occupations open to
males in the jute industry.[12] With much justification, it has
been proposed that Dundee's focus upon jute and flax had
created 'a large manufacturing centre of physically retarded
children, overworked women and demoralised men'.[13]

Although the 1860s (the decade in which John Sturrock's
diary is located) spanned some of the best years in Dundee's
modern history, the benefits were not felt evenly across the
classes. The inflow of population was at an all-time high,
while the rate of new house-building lagged far behind what
was required.[14] Sub-division of older property, much of it
medieval, and chronic overcrowding and rampant disease,
were the results. Dundee was by no means the only Victorian
city in Britain which was lacking in clean water. The extent of
its unavailability, however, a problem which was exacerbated
by the demands on an extremely limited supply made by the
burgeoning mills and factories, allied to its poor quality, were
the subjects of much critical comment and concern, and the
feeling was that Dundee's problem was worse than the rest.[15]
Even though boom conditions existed for a time as the Civil
War raged in North America (the course of which was avidly
followed by Sturrock), and fortunes were made by many of the
town's employers, the tendency was for the textile industry to

attract more workers (females in particular) and employ those who were already in the town more regularly, but without having to offer substantially higher wages.[16]

They did rise however, and conditions improved in the short-term, but sometimes with effects which did not meet with the approval of the town's middle classes. For mill and other lower paid workers, the unexpected income and the prospect of a period of full employment was a temptation to many to spend a good proportion of their windfall on drink, and 'not to be particular to be at their work on Monday morning, but . . . go in on Tuesday, or even Wednesday, or just work one week and be idle the next'.[17] Many of those so condemned were from Ireland, migrants from whence formed the largest single ethnic grouping within the textile industry and had a profound effect on the social character of Dundee.[18] Whatever their origin however, millworkers of both sexes indulged in particularly rowdy forms of street culture; where drunkenness was concerned, female millworkers were more often apprehended than males, although amongst the population at large, men were more likely to appear in the police courts than women.[19] Efforts on the part of the authorities to control drinking – by closing shebeens or arresting those involved in brawls – could incur the wrath of the mob, as happened in January 1863 when a yelling crowd of 300 'loose characters', followed and stoned the officers who had arrested two sailors for fighting, and then proceeded to smash lamps and windows in the area around the police station.[20] Rowdiness however was apparently endemic in Dundee, with its textile industry having created a far from docile army of female workers, and a 'raucous shawl-clad mill-girl culture, which shocked male observers with its coarseness and loud laughter'.[21]

Portrayed this way, in many respects Dundee seems at odds with the suggestion that Scottish Victorian towns were more likely to be better ordered than their English counterparts.[22] This however is only part of the picture, albeit a large one. It ignores the many features of Dundee's emergence as a major Scottish urban centre which it had in common with the others. Victorian Dundee presents a more complex urban phenomenon than its depiction as a 'frontier town' suggests. This is a term which is better applied to 'new' industrial towns such as Airdrie,

Coatbridge, Dalmellington and Motherwell.[23] It is quite proper that so much historical attention has been focussed on Dundee's textile industry and the conditions and culture of its female workers. Appropriately, it has been described as a 'woman's town'. Yet there was another side to the city's unbalanced economy, a world of relatively well-paid, male artisans, which at its edges at least, overlapped with that which has just been described.

John Sturrock was one of these artisans, a member of a small, elite, group, numbering some 3,000 skilled men who were employed in the twelve or so engineering firms which were going in Dundee during the 1860s. Although these men represented a variety of trades and skills, most (2,000) were workers in iron, who were said to form, 'by far the largest class of male operatives in Dundee'.[24] The companies for whom they worked made a range of metal products, including marine engines for the shipyards, and stationary steam engines for the mills and factories. The staple products upon which the sector had grown however were spinning, weaving and other machinery for the town's expanding textile industry. There was however also demand for skills in wood, in which Sturrock was competent too, for the manufacture and fitting of composite products like water wheels made at works such as the nationally-renowned Douglas Foundry, the first firm in Dundee to engage in millwright work.[25]

With only two or three firms, most notably Baxter Bros and Cox's of Lochee, being large enough to support their own engineering establishments, work for the independent foundries and engineering firms which employed millwrights such as Sturrock was plentiful during the period covered by the diary. Indeed it coincides precisely with what were probably the most prosperous years in Dundee's nineteenth century economic history. The town's textile trade, in which a pattern of boom and slump had already become established (the previous peak had been reached during the Crimean War), began to ascend new heights in the second half of 1863, as the effect of the embargo on raw cotton exports from the South during the American Civil War began to bite. Of 1864, one contemporary observed: 'High prices were ruling; large, well-appointed mills were being built; new machinery was being fitted up; [and] merchants and manufacturers were building handsome houses for themselves in the suburbs or at Broughty Ferry'.[26]

Even although the 'tide of prosperity' had ceased to flow as strongly early in 1865, ongoing commitments to new mill and factory building, and extensions to existing property, meant that the 'engineering and machine makers . . . [had] orders for months to come'.[27]

A few statistics drive the point home. Between 1864 and 1867 the number of firms in textiles increased from 61 to 72; the nominal horse-power of their steam engines rose from 4,621 to 5,822, and the spindles and powerlooms they drove from 170,550 to over 202,000, and 6,709 and 7,992 respectively. There was an accompanying rise in the number of workers, from 36,020 to 41,550.[28] In fact the engineering and millwright trades did even better than these figures suggest. For them the 1860s continued to bring prosperity, with the numbers employed almost doubling between the mid-1860s and 1871. The foundations of the good fortune of those who worked in Dundee had been laid earlier: emigration during the 1850s, and the migration of some workers to the expanding shipyards on the Clyde, had had the effect of creating a shortfall in the numbers of skilled men, 'so that although our trade is bad', noted Baxter Bros' Peter Carmichael in April 1854, 'wages are rising'.

Sturrock's diary entries reflect the buoyancy of the engineering sector: this is partly conveyed in his reports of long hours of work, until nine, ten or even eleven o'clock at night, and sometimes later, as on 19 May 1865 (and on other occasions too) when he had 'Wrought all night', as manufacturers strove to add to their stock of machinery, and repair what they already had. Significantly, several of the works at which he was employed were either being erected in 1864 and 1865, or extended.

Hard work however brought Sturrock considerable rewards, as on Saturday 1 October 1864, when he recorded that at Lilybank, and at foundries throughout Dundee, a full hour had been introduced for breakfast, without any reduction in pay. In April of the following year his wages rose by 1s., and in September by 3s., to 19s. a week, when he had expected a rise of only 2s. This was considerably more than most mill and factory workers: during the 1850s flax and jute spinners had been earning only 6s–7s.[29] By the end of 1865 Pearce Bros, the company for whom Sturrock worked, were paying their workers' wages weekly, instead of fortnightly, another valued concession, and an indication that the firm was generating a healthy cash flow.

The premises of Pearce Bros, of Lilybank Foundry, 143 Princes St, were to the north-east of the town's commercial centre, in the Cowgate. Victoria St, where Sturrock lodged until April 1865, was a few yards to the north. Both lay in the shadow of the Baxter's Dens Works, and were within sight and easy reach of the bustling docks. The most modern, the Camperdown Dock, was being hurriedly completed in 1865, in response to the demands of the town's flax and jute merchants and manufacturers for more berths for ships which had begun to import jute direct from Calcutta. Additional warehousing facilities were required too.[30] Both the final stages of its dock's construction, and the opening, marked by the entry of the colourfully-decorated, jute-laden, ship, the *George Gilroy*, were observed by Sturrock.

Although no records of Pearce Bros appear to have survived, order and time books from the later 1830s and 1840s, when the business was owned by Messrs Marshall and Edgar, serve to provide a clue as to what the nature of the business was just before Sturrock's time.[31] Marshall & Edgar employed around 70 men, who manufactured a wide range of iron castings – such as boiler plates, pulleys, brackets and block wheels – as well as making and installing flax spreading and heckling machines and spinning frames, mainly for mills and factories in and around Dundee. Railway wheels and axles were also in demand, as the Scottish railway mania ran its course. A prominent customer for mill machinery was A & D Edward, of the integrated Logie Works, which in 1864 was the second biggest in Dundee, its owners constantly in the market for the most up-to-date equipment prior to their inexplicable failure in 1876.[32] Sturrock's diary confirms that the character of the foundry's work had changed little by the mid-1860s, with several of Dundee's textile firms – Halley & Sons, John Gordon at Grove Mill in the Lower Pleasance, and

G Schelesman & Co's Balgay Mill in Lochee Rd, for example – being amongst its customers.

While it is true that in many ways, Sturrock appears to have stood apart – indeed he deliberately distanced himself – from large sections of the working classes in Dundee, particularly the 'anarchic' mill workers, there is one important sense in which he was typical of the majority of the town's inhabitants in the mid-Victorian era.

He had been born outside the town (8 November 1840), and baptised in the nearby parish of Monikie. His paternal grandfather had evidently been a small tenant farmer at Lour, near Forfar, while his father too was reputed to have been a small-scale farmer at some stage in his life. Migration towards Dundee had thus been by small steps. Sturrock's move into Dundee (the precise dating of which is uncertain) is likely to have coincided with the end of the great wave of Irish migration into the town which reached its apex in the 1840s, but carried on at a lower level through the following decade. Nevertheless, the migrant stream of which he was part, drawn from the town's rural hinterland, was that which had traditionally provided Dundee (and most of the rest of urban Scotland) with the greatest proportion of its incomers, a role which it assumed once more in the 1860s.[33] Sturrock's relatives and future wife, Anne (a distant cousin), continued to work and reside in the countryside outside Dundee. Each of his brothers (of whom there were either six or seven) were engaged in agriculture, either as the tenants of small farms, or as farm workers, although as the diary reveals, one spent at least a short (unhappy) period in the army. By providing Sturrock with a powerful incentive to return with great frequency to his roots, this may have partly softened the blow of living in the industrial city. Up until around 1850 large numbers of mill and factory workers had gone into the country during the late summer to work on the harvest.[34] The rural-urban divide was not always as sharp in practice as it may seem.[35]

Working class responses to industrialisation were many and varied. As has been widely recognised however, the radicalism of the first half of the century, which culminated in the Chartist challenge of the later 1830s and 1840s, tended to dissolve during the 1850s. Class antagonism was replaced by class collaboration, as workers came to recognise the futility of attempts to replace capitalism, and the potential benefits which the system could produce.[36] This was no less true of Dundee as it was in the other manufacturing towns of Great Britain. Former Chartists dropped out of politics, or became Liberals, and in some cases, ardent advocates of the prevailing economic system. Dundee's James Myles was one of these, who abandoned Chartist lecturing to become a bookseller, small publisher and, briefly, newspaper proprietor.[37] Thus, he declared in his *Myles Forfarshire Telegraph*, in January 1851, 'The first half of the present century is gone, and wonderful it has been', before going on to hail the triumphs of commerce and mechanical science, the praise of the last-named being heard 'in the hum of the spinning-mills, the splash of steamships, and the hissing sound of locomotives'. This was a sentiment with which Sturrock obviously had much sympathy, as will be seen below.

The principal dividing line in mid-Victorian Britain, it has been argued, was not between rich and poor, employer and employee, or capitalist and proletarian, but between those who were 'respectable' and the rest.[38] Although explanations for the cult of respectability are far from uniform, most descriptions of its features stress the importance of independence, thrift and ability to provide for one's family. Sturrock's commitment to the virtues of self-help is indicated most clearly in his accounts, which reveal not only that he saved a sizeable proportion of his earnings, but also a pattern of expenditure which included periodic contributions to the household and living expenses of members of his family, such as his mother and sisters, as well as gifts of small sums of money to various child relatives. Charitable donations – many of them spontaneously given, to the poor he passed in the street – and church door collections feature too, as they did in considerable volume throughout Dundee during the short-lived 'golden age' of the early- and mid-1860s. In 1864 one church alone raised an unprecedented £1,400 in its Christmas collection.[39]

The comfort Sturrock derived from the countryside and his kin has been noted. His church-going and pious reading (which was fairly widespread amongst self-educated working men) also provided him with succour and spiritual guidance in adverse circumstances. The cloying *Sunday Magazine*, one of his favourite pieces of reading material, provided the following fatalistic advice about how to deal with illness: if struck down,

> The first thing is to lie meek, and humble, and still. If you are tempted to murmur at times wasted, or opportunities lost, remember that He, who has bidden you to redeem the time, must know the value of it better than you . . . Hymns at such times are a great solace . . . If the message comes that the Master calls for you, to depart and be with Christ, if worse for us, is better for you.

His enthusiasm for sermons, which regularly took him into two different churches on a Sunday, confirms the notion of the God-fearing Scottish presbyterian artisan[40], and underlines the religiosity of the urban Scot.[41] He was fervently anti-Catholic too, dismissing a Christmas Day mass he attended in St Mary's RC church as 'the merest piece of trumpery that I ever saw'. Instead, he enthused about his attendance at a soiree of the Scottish Reformation Society – for which he paid entry money of 1s. – which was one of a number of organisations established in the nineteenth century in Scotland to protect the country from the 'dangers' of Catholicism.[42] Protestant martyrs, notably John Knox, were amongst his heroes.

He identified too with the emergent Scottish nationalism of the mid-nineteenth century – a 'particular form of patriotism which recreated Scotland as a nation within a nation'[43] – not only reading Sir Walter Scott's poems, but also visiting and making a small donation to the partially completed Wallace Monument on Abbey Craig, near Stirling, which he took the opportunity to visit when he was working temporarily in the area repairing the shafting in the Hillfoots mill of the woollen manufacturers Alexander Wilson & Co.[44] Another trip into the country – this time strictly for leisure purposes, at the start of his annual holiday – took him by rail to Pitlochry ('Pitlochrie' in the original), and thereafter to Killiecrankie, another symbol of a Scottish identity which drew on the Lowlanders' incorporation of the romanticised Highlands (reinforced by their adoption by Queen Victoria and Prince Albert) and a neutered Jacobitism. There was almost certainly a self-improving aspect to his excursion.[45] Significantly, given the contemporary vogue on the part of some paternalistic employers to encourage loyalty and encourage their workers to participate in 'rational' leisure pursuits, of which the excursion train was one, a week earlier Sturrock had watched as a party of Carron Iron Works employees passed through Perth station, *en route* for Blair Atholl.

As has been suggested, Sturrock was in many respects the archetypal 'respectable' working man, who embodied the evangelical culture of urban Britain which 'deprecated idle or useless leisure'.[46] This can be seen in the opening paragraph of the diary, which is a statement of his motives for keeping it. Amongst other things, Sturrock was anxious to 'form an estimate' of how he spent his time away from work, and ascertain whether he had been 'trifling it away or turning it to any particular advantage.' His habits and attitudes were the antithesis of the sorts of working class behaviour which so distressed contemporaries in Dundee and elsewhere; particularly loathsome were young workers from the mills and factories, who instead of spending their evenings pursuing 'intellectual and moral culture, and healthful and harmless amusements and recreations', congregated on the streets. These, it was claimed, were 'generally crowded with the youth of both sexes, and immodest songs, obscene language, oaths, and curses, are too frequently heard, and that as often from the gentler sex as from the other'.[47]

Sturrock too recoiled from such sights, as on one evening late in February 1865 when he wandered into the town's swarming Overgate district, but was quickly driven out by the 'smell of spirits and tobacco', and perhaps more in a part of Dundee which was renowned for its drunkenness, poverty and prostitution. He was however prepared to go to the circus, and to the 'shows' which accompanied the town's annual July fair, and although disapproving on the first occasion, on the second, the following year (1865), he lingered longer and indeed stopped and talked to some weavers, female factory operatives who were said to be a hard-working, thrifty and self-respecting class of workers.[48] By the 1860s, these were mainly females, powerloom weavers who had replaced male handloom weavers from the early 1840s, and who tended to stand apart from the rather more noisy and less restrained spinners and preparers in the 'low' mills.

This was about as far as he was prepared to go in a life which was singularly short of abandon: an exception seems to have been the traditional Hallowe'en celebration, an enduring event in Scotland's somewhat restricted but far from moribund calendar of popular festivity.[49] In November 1864 he was evidently involved in a night-time trip to an open air reel in Baxter Park, while he was also present at a spontaneous and spirited Hallowe'en dance on 13 November 1865, when with a dozen or so friends, Sturrock 'went out and got hold of a blind fiddler' to provide the music. That he was later able to attend to his accounts suggest that this was a sober, if energetic, affair. Indeed expenditure on alcohol is notable by its virtual absence from Sturrock's list of outlays; only occasionally did he indulge in a glass of wine or a modest quantity of porter (although on one occasion, 28 December 1865, he did buy two pints). Whisky consumption was evidently confined to weddings.

Nor does his diary provide the slightest suggestion of sexual impropriety. Not for him the abuse of their status and some-times workplace power by male mill overseers, mechanics and others in skilled occupations, who found themselves pursued in the Sheriff Court by the distressed mothers of illegitimate and unsupported infants, with the date and precise location of the site of the alleged conception – as on a 'common stair in Brown St, Westport, Dundee' – publicly revealed.[50] Despite the increasing dependence of households in Dundee on the earnings of females, and the existence of many more female heads of households than was the norm elsewhere, Sturrock shared the dominant Victorian ideology as far as women were concerned, which rested on the notions of 'separate spheres' and the chastity (before marriage) of women.[51] His ideal, of a domestic angel and supportive companion (as well as other suitable attributes, outlined in publications such as the *Sunday Magazine*), was represented by Anne, to whom he was devoted, and married in December 1867, and who, he hoped (29 October 1864), would relieve him of the tedious task of sewing his clothes.

Self-consciously he battled with indolence, reprimanding himself if he lay in bed later than nine o'clock on a Sunday morning. One of the most interesting days he had, 15 January 1865, which he spent walking and exploring in and around Stirling, was marred because it was a Sunday, and he had neglected his usual religious devotions. He was a regular attender at the Watt Institute, Dundee's mechanics institute which had originally opened in 1824 for the use of 'young tradesmen in the useful branches of arts and sciences'. Although numbers attending had fallen off by mid-century, Sturrock was a regular attender at a revived series of lectures held at new premises in Lindsay St.[52] At the Library there, and in his lodgings he spent hours both in the evenings and at weekends reading useful and improving literature, which mass production had made much more readily available. In the cases of the *Dundee Advertiser* and the weekly *People's Journal*, both of which he purchased regularly, Sturrock was one of the early beneficiaries of the removal of the Stamp Tax in 1855, which heralded what has been described as a 'revolution' in popular publishing.[53] Sturrock was thus able to enjoy, in the columns of the *Advertiser*, the serialised novels of David Pae, an immensely popular writer who emphasised the need for personal moral reform – amongst all classes.[54]

Arithmetical exercises and engineering drawing were staple ingredients of the leisure hours he spent indoors. In studying subjects which were work-related, Sturrock was unlike most self-educated artisans, whose search for 'useful knowledge' usually took them towards more heady works of literature and philosophy.[55] Sturrock however was not entirely uninterested in these disciplines, and read the poetry of Crabbe, Milton and the aforementioned Scott.

Apparently keener to please than most respectable but staunchly independent artisans, and showing little of the suspicion of middle-class patronage and guidance which evidently characterised the labour aristocrats in Kentish Town and Edinburgh[56], Sturrock's reading matter would have greatly impressed those employers in Dundee who shared Peter Carmichael's belief that young men (apprentices in particular) should be advised of the 'advantages of education' and the 'disgrace of ignorance'. In order to compete with their continental rivals, firms like his required educated workers: thus, he counselled, 'Lads beginning their apprenticeship should be encouraged in every possible way to continue their education in the evening'.[57] This however appears to have been a minority view, with most training still being obtained by practice and example.[58]

One of the books Sturrock read however, William Templeton's popular *The Millwrights' and Engineers' Pocket Companion* (1833), boasted that it distinguished itself from much of the rest of the genre, which had been 'swelled out by theoretical problems'. It contained much practical information, with sections on the strength of materials, specific gravities, and geometry, as well as descriptions and capacities of various sorts of water and steam pumping and other engines. Less obviously useful, but typical of the eclectic reading habits of the self-taught, he periodically digested chunks of Chambers' popular and cheap *Encyclopaedia*. Scottish works of this sort however, with their overt moral overtones, should not be confused with their colder, less 'human', English counterparts[59], one of which, the *English Mechanic*, he began to purchase, in instalments, in October 1865.

Yet despite the apparent closeness of the relationship between Sturrock and his employers – indicated in his numerous visits to the house of his manager, John Sturrock[60] – he also had a strong foothold in working-class society. The *Advertiser* was solidly Liberal, while even more radical was the reforming *People's Journal*, which had the biggest circulation of any weekly paper outside London. There is no sign that Sturrock ever bought the Tory *Courier*. What this suggests is that he shared the political culture of the skilled, male Scottish working classes[61], and was in sympathy with the Abolitionist, pro-North stand which the *People's Journal*'s editor, William Latto, took during the American Civil War. Latto had been a Chartist, and a handloom weaver.[62] Radicalism in this context however should not be confused with class antagonism: sympathetic to labour, Dundee's Liberal newspapers were resolutely committed to the causes of amelioration and reconciliation.[63] Sturrock however had more specific reasons to be interested in the Civil War (although he had a genuine fascination in America and American culture) in that he had relatives there, two of whom died as a result of the conflict.

As has been seen, Sturrock shared too the enthusiasm for

nationalist movements which periodically fired the political consciousness of the skilled working class in Scotland. This was international in scope, as can be seen by his enthusiasm for the preaching of the Rev. Alessando Gavazzi, the Italian patriot and republican, whose combination of nationalist ardour and anti-papal rhetoric evidently had a powerful appeal for Sturrock. Popular Liberalism in Dundee, tapped and reinforced by the local press, was, as in many other British towns, both intensely local *and* international in its outlook.[64] In Dundee however, it has been argued that provincialism predominated.[65] This however should not be allowed to conceal the commitment of many Dundonians to the empire, seen in part by the Volunteer movement which was born in Dundee in 1859.[66] Amongst those who had joined Dundee's 1st Volunteer Battalion of the Royal Highlanders was Sturrock's fellow-lodger, Mungo Smith.

Further confirmation of his place within the mainstream of that segment of the working class described above is found in Sturrock's devotion to the lectures (organised through the Watt Institute) of the Rev. George Gilfillan, another radical Liberal, whose attacks on the worst of the iniquities of industrialism were also tempered by his acceptance of the capitalist order.[67]

As far as the current debate about the nature of social relations in nineteenth century Britain is concerned, Sturrock provides no support for those who favour coercion or social control as explanations for the absence of conflict.[68] Indeed, while the diary provides few clues to the formative influences upon Sturrock prior to 1864, there can be little doubt that this was a man who not only consented to the capitalist system, but who positively revelled in its bounties.

In this he was not alone.[69] Reference has already been made to James Myles. Another example is Ellen Johnston, for several years a powerloom weaver in Dundee, and a near-contemporary of Sturrock, who wrote and published a series of what to modern eyes read as cloying and sycophantic poems in praise of particular factories, employers and managers.[70] 'Dear Chapelshade Factory! Once more do I hail thee', is the first line of her poem, 'Most Respectfully Dedicated to Mr James Dorward', a weaving manager at Chapershade works, and is indicative of the form and tone. What is important is that recent work which has begun to look behind the assumptions long made about the part played by class consciousness in determining working class identity in mid-Victorian Britain suggests that Johnston may have been more representative of working class attitudes generally than might be assumed.[71] So too might John Sturrock. Further investigation into class formation and relations in Victorian Dundee however is required before a definitive answer can be given.

Of several factors which account for the accommodation of the working class in Victorian Scotland with capitalism, one which may have been particularly influential in Sturrock's case was the material circumstances in which he found himself. Above all there was his skilled occupation, with its irregular hours (except for Saturdays, when he usually finished at 2 pm), and the absence of close supervision, which contrasted with the tedium and regimented nature of much mill and factory work (see entry for 4 January 1865). There was too the variety of tasks upon which he was engaged, and the different locations at which he was employed, and of course the relatively high wages he was paid. He was no proletarian, suffering indignities such as loss of status, and the low pay, which accompanied 'de-skilling'.[72] Sturrock by contrast was able to afford to fund a lifestyle which included luxuries such as fruit and sweets, refreshments, newspapers, journals and books, a fair amount of travel by rail and cab, and various other forms of commercial entertainment, in the form of shows and the occasional visit to a diorama. Sturrock was fortunate enough to be able to afford to buy the medicine and castor oil which was recommended as the cure for his racking cough in May 1865.

Sturrock benefited too from the bourgeois assault within and beyond the workplace, at the heart of which was the paternalist model of industrial relations. Although relatively little research has been done on this in Scotland[73], it is certain that such a strategy was adopted by some Scottish employers.[74] Dundee was not excluded, although the absence of investigation into the extent and nature of employer paternalism in the dominant textile industry means that the picture is currently both impressionistic and patchy.

Sturrock's diary shows that his employers, Pearce Bros, used a paternalist style of management, paying an unexpected wage rise for example (see above), and organising a supper at the

Albion Hotel (18 August 1865) to celebrate the completion of a particular contract. That their methods bore fruit can be seen in Sturrock's attendance (16 November 1865) at a worker-sponsored soiree in the Thistle Hall, held to give thanks to Pearce Bros for their decision to pay wages weekly rather than fortnightly. Events like this do not appear to have been unusual, even in the textile industry. In mid-century, firms such as J & W Brown, of the East Mill, and Brown & Millar, were also in the habit of holding socials at which tea and cakes and other foodstuffs were served, and where both employees and proprietors were present.[75] It should not be assumed however that the pressures to conform were all coming from 'above': workers as well as employers had as much if not more of a vested interest in co-operation as they had in conflict.[76]

As has just been suggested, the bounds of paternalism extended beyond the factory gate, in what amounted to a 'cultural offensive'.[77] The crisis confronting the employing classes in Dundee in the 1830s and 1840s, referred to above, had a transforming effect on their actions not unlike that which prevailed amongst their much more closely-scrutinised counterparts in towns such as Bradford, England's fastest growing textile town in the early nineteenth century.[78] There, social dislocation, civic squalor, alienation and political challenge had led to the industrial bourgeoisie 'taming social, cultural, and environmental forces that by the 1830s seemed beyond control'.[79] In a relatively short period of time, confrontation was replaced by liberal consensus.

Similarly, it was reported in Dundee in 1850, while great extremes of wealth and poverty still existed side by side, during the previous ten years the town's 'influential classes', who included several leading employers, had 'exerted themselves in the promotion of schemes of benevolence for the exclusive benefit of working men, with a view to increasing their comforts and elevating their characteristics'. It was anticipated that these measures, which had included the provision of coffee and reading rooms, model lodging houses, ragged schools and allotments, would result in a 'better feeling springing up between the different ranks of society', which in turn would 'tend to assuage popular discontent, and increase the general happiness of the community'.[80]

By the early 1860s, the process of reform had gone even further, although not always with the enthusiasm that some of the town's mercantile elite would have wished. Appalled at the state of Dundee's water and sewerage arrangements, which had resulted in another outbreak of cholera in 1853, Peter Carmichael declared that 'our present liberty is licentiousness', and that he would rather 'live under a despotism for a few years', than witness further the consequences of foul water, along with shortfalls in educational provision. Amelioration on the scale that was required was slow in coming. Civic improvement in Dundee, as in many British towns, lagged behind Glasgow. Many mill and factory proprietors were evidently solid supporters of and contributors to the Calvinist view which pervaded bourgeois Scotland, namely that to intervene and tackle the causes of diseases such as cholera would be to interfere with God's purpose, and raise rates. (Carmichael's explanation for the lack of action on Dundee's water problem in 1853 was that 'No-one will allow his pocket to be touched'.) Changing minds was a slow process which required reformers to appeal more to self-interest than to the worthiness of their cause.[81] Yet such was the extent of the squalor which they saw before them that some philanthropic individuals were driven to abandon the ideology of inaction.

Although the moves to municipal improvement did not gather much force until the 1870s and 1880s, enough had been done by 1864 to enable John Sturrock, in common with similarly placed working men in many parts of Britain, to take advantage of several of the private and philanthropic improvements referred to above.[82] He visited the Dock Street Refreshment Rooms, for example, and on other occasions drank coffee in coffee rooms; periodically he had a warm bath at the public baths at West Protection Wall.

Sturrock's favourite leisure activity however, which he usually engaged in several times a week, was walking, sitting and musing in Baxter Park, which was situated within a few hundred yards of his lodgings. On the personal level this makes sense. Sturrock's father, William, was by the time of the diary, a gardener, and keeper of the Panmure Monument on the estate of the same name, and he may therefore have been in a better position than most urban workers to appreciate the 'walks [which] existed in

all directions. . . . between beautiful shrubberies and beds of rare
and lovely flowers', although it has been argued, perhaps with
too little qualification, that the 'love of gardens and gardening
was one of the few tastes which many Victorians of all social
conditions had in common'.[83]

Gardens however had been widely used in the Scottish mor-
alists' crusade to provide 'systematic recreation' for the working
classes.[84] Diary entries too confirm that Sturrock found great
pleasure in taking advantage of the park's elevated location, as
well as the town's recently laid-out Eastern Necropolis. From
Baxter Park, contemporaries believed, the 'finest' view of the
Tay estuary could be had.[85]

While the laying out of parks and pleasure gardens was
not new in the nineteenth century, the creation of 'useful
landscapes within the town for the use and enjoyment of the
public at large' was 'essentially a Victorian idea'[86], inspired
by the rapid growth of unhealthy, air-less industrial cities,
concern about 'rational recreation' and the desire to create
'places of innocent amusement where people could mix and
enjoy the beauty of the flowers and trees and in so doing
become virtuous and happy.'[87] This was certainly so with
Dundee's Baxter Park, whose paternalist sponsors anticipated
that it provided 'the working population [of Dundee] with a
means of recreation and enjoyment after their hard labour and
honest industry'.[88] Class tensions (but not class distinctions)
were to be dissolved on this 'common ground, where all
the inhabitants of that large and busy town may meet in
mutual acknowledgement of their dependence the one upon
the other.'

Much of the impetus for the provision of parks came from
the local authorities, notably in the Scottish case from Glasgow
Town Council.[89] Less important overall, but of particular
importance in the 1860s, was the thrust which the movement
derived from local benefactors, such as industrialists like Titus
Salt at Saltaire, or Sir Francis Crossley in Halifax. See too
Cunningham. Similarly in Dundee, Baxter Park, the fourth
of the great public parks to be laid out in Scotland in the
nineteenth century (after others in Edinburgh and Glasgow),
was the gift of David Baxter, of Baxter Bros. Designed by the
country's leading landscape architect, Sir Joseph Paxton, it

was opened to the public in September 1863, to the acclaim
of a massive crowd of an estimated 70,000 people.[90]

Parks also provided controlled space for marking events of
major local, national or even international significance. Baxter
Park played host to some of these. One instance was the Queen's
Birthday in May 1865, which was celebrated by a performance
by an Artillery Band, and watched by Sturrock. The order of
this occasion contrasts with the apparent disorder of earlier
celebrations of this sort, as on the Queen's Birthday in 1853,
which had culminated in the sacking of the Town House and the
breaking of virtually every window in the High Street. Indeed it
was this outrage, which came as a profound shock to a number of
contemporaries, which strengthened the campaign in Dundee
for more leisure space: 'You cannot coop up hordes of human
beings in narrow pestilential closes, hemmed in on all sides
with whisky shops, and pawn shops', stormed the *Advertiser*,
without regard to their 'social condition', including housing.
Extended church provision and the exhortations of ministers
were of little avail. Other large towns, the paper went on, had
parks and botanical and zoological gardens: 'If amusements are
not provided . . . they may be expected to amuse themselves,
and that occasionally, without much consideration for public
order and quiet'.[91] Remarkably, less than twenty years later,
the generosity of Dundee's provision of public leisure grounds
was a matter of envy in some quarters.[92]

Yet even by Sturrock's time, Baxter Park was by no means the
only part of Dundee through which he could apparently travel
unmolested, with nothing untoward to offend his sensibilities.
(By and large, he appears to have been immune to the
concentrations of squalor which scarred Dundee prior to the
first major wave of slum clearance and road widening which
followed the Improvement Act of 1871.) The Overgate was
clearly an exception, and it would be flying in the face of the
evidence to ignore the incidence of drunkenness and endemic
disorder in Victorian Dundee, but even so, Marine Parade,
Stannergate, Cowgate, Bucklemaker Wynd (Hilltown), High
St, Murraygate, Nethergate, Blackness Rd, Perth Rd and
Magdalene Green and were all relatively quiet, at least at
the times when Sturrock chose to walk through them. It
was during what were typically shortlived strikes that the

town's commercial centre was invaded by hooting, chanting, gesticulating females[93], but 1864 and 1865 were good years for industrial relations. Although 'promenading' on the town's main thoroughfares in the evenings was a notorious feature of the boisterous leisure habits of mill and factory workers in the evenings, this did not go on much after 9 pm; it was on Saturday nights that things tended to get 'rough' and out of hand. Sturrock spent most of his Saturday evenings ensconced in his lodgings, reading and writing, or in the country.[94]

This 'Introduction' is not intended to be exhaustive. Readers will have their own interests to follow, and will explore avenues which are not mapped out here. It is to be hoped that like Sturrock, who walked many more miles in a typical week than most twentieth century urban dwellers do in months, and who as a consequence frequented his cobbler's premises in Victoria Street with a frequency which today seems uncanny, their journeys will be fulfilling.

NOTES

1. J. Burnett, *Useful Toil* (London, 1974), p. 10.
2. The originals of these are held in the Archives Department, University of Dundee, MS 15/58/1, Vols 1 and 2 of John Sturrock's Diaries, 15 August 1864–19 November 1865; MS 15/58/2, John Sturrock's Account of Income and Expenditure, 1865. The diary and accounts are reproduced here largely in the typescript form into which they were put by his grandson, although the original copy of the accounts appears to have been lost. He corrected and modernised Sturrock's spelling and inadequate grammar. Unfortunately this does have the effect of removing some of the immediacy of the original and gives the impression that Sturrock was a rather better writer than he really was. On the other hand, reproduced this way the text is much easier to follow, and little of substance is lost. Readers intending to quote from the diary however should still quote from the original. Minor errors in Sturrock's arithmetic have also been corrected, but even so a small imbalance between income and expenditure remains.
3. D. Vincent, *Bread, Knowledge and Freedom: A Study of Nineteenth-Century Working Class Autobiography* (London, 1981), p. 8.
4. See C. A. Whatley, 'Images of Dundee: Fact, Fiction and

Function in the Works of Victorian Working Class Writers in Dundee' (unpublished paper); for discussion of the literary genre within which Myles worked, see W. Donaldson, *Popular Literature in Victorian Scotland* (Aberdeen, 1986).

5. Vincent, *Bread, Knowledge and Freedom*, p. 131.
6. On Dundee's economic development in the first half of the nineteenth century, see S. G. E. Lythe, 'The Historical Background', in J. M. Jackson (ed), *The Third Statistical Account of Scotland: The City of Dundee* (Arbroath, 1979), pp. 69–76; G. Jackson and K. Kinnear, *The Trade and Shipping of Dundee, 1780–1850* (Dundee, 1991); C. A. Whatley, 'The Making of "Juteopolis" – and How it Was', in C. A. Whatley (ed), *The Remaking of Juteopolis: Dundee c.1891–1991* (Dundee, 1992), pp. 7–22.
7. Dundee Archive and Record Centre, Town Council General Committee Minute Books, 1839–1843, Vol. 3.
8. G. Lewis, *The Filth and Fever Bills of Dundee, and What Might be Made of Them* (Dundee, 1841), pp. 3–5.
9. Whatley, 'The Making', p. 12.
10. R. Rodger, 'Employment, Wages and Poverty in the Scottish Cities, 1841–1914', in G. Gordon (ed), *Perspectives of the Scottish City* (Aberdeen, 1985), pp. 40–1.
11. See B. Lenman, C. Lythe and E. Gauldie, *Dundee and its Textile Industry, 1850–1914* (Dundee, 1969).
12. D. Lennox, 'Working Class Life in Dundee for 25 years, 1878 to 1903' (unpublished thesis, 2 vols, c.1906, University of Dundee), I, pp. 169–70; Dundee Social Union, *Report on Housing and Industrial Conditions* (Dundee, 1905), pp. 49–55; O. Gordon, *Handbook of Employments* (Aberdeen, 1908), pp. 99–104.
13. W. M. Walker, *Juteopolis: Dundee and its textile workers, 1885–1923* (Edinburgh, 1979), p. 85.
14. Lenman, Lythe and Gauldie, *Dundee Textile Industry*, pp. 77–102.
15. Ibid, pp. 8–9, 77.
16. Ibid, pp. 64, 67, 70.
17. *Dundee Advertiser*, 31 July 1863.
18. B. E. Collins, Aspects of Irish immigration into two Scottish towns (Dundee and Paisley) during the mid-nineteenth century (unpublished M. Phil. thesis, University of Edinburgh, 1979), pp. 48, 235–7.
19. C. Bull, 'Who Are the Subalternists? A Study of the Dundee Millworkers from 1850–1885' (unpublished M. Phil. thesis, University of St Andrews, 1989), pp. 19–31.
20. *Dundee Advertiser*, 27 January 1863.

21. R. J. Morris, 'Urbanisation and Scotland', in W. H. Fraser and R. J. Morris (eds), *People and Society in Scotland, Volume II, 1830–1914* (Edinburgh, 1990), p. 80; for a fuller account, see E. Gordon, *Women and the Labour Movement in Scotland, 1850–1914* (Oxford, 1991), pp. 137–168.

22. Morris, 'Urbanisation', p. 91; see too G. F. A. Best, 'Another Part of the Island: Some Scottish Perspectives', in H. J. Dyos and M. Wolff (eds), *The Victorian City: Images and Realities* (London, 1978), pp. 389–411.

23. For recent studies of some of these communities, see A. Campbell, *The Lanarkshire Miners* (Edinburgh, 1979), and R. Duncan, *Steelopolis: The Making of Motherwell c.*1750–1939 (Motherwell, 1991).

24. Dundee District Libraries, Lamb Collection, 278 (5), 'Iron Trades', c.1872.

25. Dundee District Libraries, Lamb Collection, 196 (46), *The Reformer*, 9 December 1871.

26. University of Dundee Archives, MS 102/1/2, Peter Carmichael's 'Life and Letters', p. 270.

27. Ibid, p. 293.

28. See A. J. Warden, *The Linen Trade, Ancient and Modern* (London, 1867 ed), and M. Watson, *Jute and Flax Mills in Dundee* (Tayport, 1990).

29. Rodger, 'Employment', p. 41.

30. C. A. Whatley, D. B. Swinfen and A. M. Smith, *The Life and Times of Dundee* (Edinburgh, 1993), p. 80.

31. University of Dundee Archives, MS 46/1, Marshall & Edgar, Order Book, 1836–47, and MS 46/2, Time Book, 1846–7.

32. Watson, *Jute And Flax Mills*, p. 23.

33. M. W. Flinn (ed), *Scottish Population History* (Cambridge, 1977), pp. 466–7.

34. Lenman, Lythe and Gauldie, *Textile Industry*, p. 57.

35. For a telling example, see Dundee District Council, Archive and Record Centre, GD/x99/10, Memoir of Alexander Moncur.

36. There are many books on the subject of the so-called 'Mid-Victorian consensus'. A useful introduction is D. G. Wright, *Popular Radicalism: The Working-Class Experience 1780–1880* (London, 1988), pp. 150–69; on Scotland see W. Knox, 'The Political and Workplace Culture of the Scottish Working-Class', in Fraser and Morris, *People and Society, Vol II*, pp. 138–66.

37. W. Norrie, *Dundee Celebrities of the Nineteenth Century*

(Dundee, 1873), pp. 132–3; see too L. C. Wright, *Scottish Chartism* (edinburgh, 1953), p. 210.

38. G. Best, *Mid-Victorian Britain, 1851–1875* (London, 1971), p. 260.
39. *Dundee Advertiser,* 26 December 1984.
40. C. Brown, *The People in the Pews: Religion and Society in Scotland Since 1780* (Studies in Scottish Economic & Social History, Glasgow 1993), p. 31.
41. Morris, 'Urbanisation', p. 92.
42. E. W. McFarland, *Protestants First: Orangeism in* 19th Century Scotland (Edinburgh, 1990), pp. 96–101.
43. R. J. Morris, 'Victorian Values in Scotland and England', in T. C. Smout (ed), *Victorian Values* (Oxford, 1992), p. 38.
44. For a general account of nationalism in Scotland, see H. J. Hanham, *Scottish Nationalism* (London, 1969), and for cultural aspects of this, see M. G. H. Pittock, *The Invention of Scotland: The Stuart Myth and Scottish Identity, 1638 to the Present* (London, 1991).
45. H. Cunningham, *Leisure in the Industrial Revolution* (London, 1980), pp. 158–9.
46. Brown, *The People in the Pews,* p. 32.
47. Dundee District Libraries, Lamb Collection, 196ᵃ (25), 'The Trades of Dundee', newspaper cutting, nd, c.1856.
48. The best recent description and analysis of the weavers' characteristics and culture is to be found in E. Gordon, *Women and the Labour Movement in Scotland* 1850–1914 (Oxford, 1991), pp. 155–8; see too Walker, 1979, *Juteopolis,* pp. 43–4.
49. W. H. Fraser, 'Developments in Leisure', in Fraser and Morris, *People and Society Vol. II,* p. 250.
50. Information gleaned from the much-neglected Sheriff Court records; for 1863–4, see Scottish Record Office, Dundee Sheriff Court, SC 45/1/12.
51. For a recent survey see E. Gordon, 'Women's Spheres', in Fraser and Morris, *People and Society Vol. II,* pp. 206–35.
52. J. Paul, 'Scientific and Literary Institutions', in A. W. Paton and A. H. Millar (eds), *Handbook and Guide to Dundee and District* (Dundee, 1912), p. 408.
53. W. Donaldson, *Popular Literature in Victorian Scotland* (Aberdeen, 1986), p. 2.
54. Ibid, pp. 87–95.
55. Vincent, *Bread, Knowledge and Freedom,* p. 135.
56. See Wright, *Popular Radicalism,* p. 167; J. Belchem, *Industrialisation and the Working Class: The English Experience,*

1750–1900 (Aldershot, 1990), p. 173, and others deny that 'embourgeoisement' or 'assimilation of middle-class values' was involved as the working classes carved their identity in mid-Victorian Britain. While allowing that Sturrock's independent habits and attitudes may have been generated from within his own class, he seems not to have been entirely free of 'deferential respectability'. Values were shared. See Knox, 'Political and Workplace Culture', pp. 152–61.

57. University of Dundee Archives, Peter Carmichael's 'Life and Letters', pp. 145–8.
58. Vincent, *Bread, Knowledge and Freedom*, p. 142.
59. Morris, 'Victorian Values', pp. 35–6.
60. John Sturrock was listed in the *Dundee Directory* of 1864–5 as manager of Lilybank Foundry. He lived close by, in fact in the same street. He may have been a distant relative of Sturrock, but if so the diary makes no reference to this.
61. Knox, 'Political and Workplace Culture', p. 152.
62. Donaldson, *Popular Literature*, p. 98.
63. This was not unique either to Dundee or Scotland. See P. Joyce, *Visions of the People: Industrial England and the Question of Class*, 1848–1914 (Cambridge, 1991), pp. 40–3.
64. Ibid, p. 41.
65. D. Dunn, 'Dundee Considered as Mount Parnassus', in W. N. Herbert and R. Price (eds), *Gairfish: A Dundee Anthology* (Dundee, 1991), pp. 40–2.
66. See H. T. Templeman, 'What Dundee Contributes to the Empire', in Paton and Millar, *Handbook and Guide*.
67. Walker, *Juteopolis*, pp. 53–4.
68. For an excellent survey, see A. J. Reid, *Social Classes and Social Relations in Britain*, 1850–1914 (London, 1992).
69. Knox, 'Political and Workplace Culture', p. 158.
70. E. Johnston, *Autobiography: Poems and Songs of Ellen Johnston, The 'Factory Girl'* (Glasgow, 1867).
71. P. Joyce, 'A people and a class: industrial workers and the social order in nineteenth-century England', in M. L. Bush (ed), *Social Orders and Social Classes in Europe Since 1500* (London, 1992), pp. 199–217.
72. Joyce, 'A people and a class', pp. 203–4.
73. The classic English study is P. Joyce, *Work, Society & Politics: the culture of the factory in later Victorian England* (London, 1992 ed).
74. Knox, 'Political and Workplace Culture', p. 143; J. McG. Davies, 'Social and Labour Relations at Pullars of Perth,

1882–1924', *Scottish Economic & Social History*, Vol. 13 (1993), pp. 27–42.

75. *Myles' Forfarshire Telegraph*, 4 January 1851.
76. Joyce, 'A People and a Class', pp. 204–5.
77. Joyce, *Visions of the People*, p. 59.
78. T. Koditschek, *Class Formation and Urban Industrial Society: Bradford, 1750–1850* (Cambridge, 1990).
79. The words are from J. A. Epstein, review of Koditschek, in *International Labour and Working Class History*, 42 (Fall 1992), p. 106.
80. J. Myles, *Rambles in Forfarshire, or Sketches in Town and Country* (Dundee, 1850), p. xiii.
81. See A. A. MacLaren, 'Bourgeois Ideology and Victorian Philanthropy: The Contradictions of Cholera', in A. A. Maclaren (ed), *Social Class in Scotland: Past and Present* (Edinburgh, 1976), pp. 36–54.
82. Belchem, *Industrialisation and the Working Class*, pp. 171–5.
83. J. Carre, 'The Public Park', in B. Ford (ed), *Victorian Britain* (Cambridge, 1992 ed), p. 77.
84. Fraser, 'Developments in Leisure', p. 244.
85. Dundee District Libraries, Lamb Collection, 228 (20), *Handbook to the Places of Public Recreation in Dundee*, nd, pp. 1–3.
86. G. F. Chadwick, *The Park and the Town: Public Landscape in the* 19th and 20th Centuries (London, 1966), p. 19.
87. H. Conway, *People's Parks: The Design and Development of Victorian Parks in Britain* (Cambridge, 1991), p. 202.
88. University of Dundee Archives, MS 105/XI/1, Minute Book (Vol. 1) of Baxter Park, 1863–1901, p. 4.
89. Conway, *People's Parks*, pp. 57–8.
90. Whatley, Swinfen and Smith, *Life and Times of Dundee*, p. 119.
91. *Dundee Advertiser*, 7 June 1853.
92. Dundee District Libraries, Lamb Collection, 228 (21), newspaper cutting (1871) from the *Sheffield Telegraph*.
93. Gordon, *Women Workers*, pp. 177–8.
94. Ibid, pp. 162–3; Lennox, 'Working Class Life', p. 286.

I

THE DIARY OF
JOHN STURROCK

sleepy by that time I went to my
bed [about] seven and lay till a
quarter to nine next morning

Uncle Day went along in the fore
-noon to my Brother Davidson at Panmure
and then to Alexanders at Guildy who
I am sorry to say has been laid up for
five weeks now with a rheumatic fever
and little or no prospect of being anything
any better yet. Went back to the
[Monument?] again and started for
the [Kelleas?] at three oclock where I
arrived about half five and got my
tea with Anne and her Father
with us home I spent part of the evening
most happily. Then went up with
Anne and her Brother James and
his wife to their house where we
spent another two or three hours most
delightfully and got to bed about
twelve o'clock

6 Spent the whole forenoon one way
or other here and stopped at [Inglis?]
for my Brother Williams at George
-[town?] Cassingle called on Robert
Sturrock at Liverclyst as I passed
where I got dinner then on his Brother
Alexander and his Mother who was

Page from Sturrock's diary.
University of Dundee Archives, MS 15/58/1.

VICTORIA STREET, DUNDEE, AUGUST 15TH 1864.

Having commenced work in Lilybank Foundry here in Dundee today, I have resolved to keep a sort of journal or register of how I spend my leisure time, as much perhaps from curiosity as any other thing, but as I intend to keep a true and faithful record of how I spend and where I spend every evening, together with some of the more particular occurrences of my daily life, also my correspondence, thoughts and feelings, and any particular mood or frame of mind I may be in, I may be able to form an estimate of how I have spent my leisure time, whether I have been trifling it away or turning it to any particular advantage. This first evening, August 15, I have spent at home reading the newspapers and resolving in my mind how I was to head this.

TUES. 16. Called on an aunt of my father's, Mrs McHardy, and also her daughter, Mrs Arthur, with whom I spent the evening.

WED. 17. Called on Mrs and Misses Packman. Went to Baxter Park with Elizabeth, also Helen Wright, with whom I went home.

THURS. 18. Spent the evening in cleaning drawing tools and reading Chambers *Encyclopaedia*.

FRI. 19. Had a visit from John Wright tonight, after which wrote a letter to Anne Sturrock, Kellas, and must now hasten to bed for it is past one o'clock.

SAT. 20. Went down to the railway station with my father in the afternoon. Then went and took a stroll through the new docks which are being made at present. Went round the harbour and took a look at the shipping. Came home to tea about six o'clock. Went in the town again for an hour or two. Put eight pounds in the bank and bought an album for holding portraits in.

SUN. 21. Took a walk in the Baxter Park this morning before breakfast. Went to Wallacetown Free Church in the forenoon, Free St Andrews in the afternoon. Read a while after tea Hawes's

Commentary on the Song of Solomon and Mr Charles's letter. Went through the Park again and out Stobsmuir Road and happened to meet Margaret Packman with whom I came home and have spent about two hours in idle gossip which might have been employed in useful reading.

MON. 22. Went to the town on some small errands where I spent the greater part of the evening.

TUES. 23. Spent the evening at home in reading and arithmetic. Annoyed about an hour with a young lass, for whose company I had no relish.

WED. 24. Called on Mr and Mrs Peter Kydd with whom I once lodged. Spent about an hour coming home in looking at the auctioneers on the High Street and could not help thinking that were one to hear them, without seeing or knowing what they were, one would not believe that they were other than a pack of madmen.

THURS. 25. Working tonight till a quarter to nine o'clock.

FRI. 26. Dundee Fair and annual holidays. Happened to meet Margaret Wright tonight with whom I went along to Ward Foundry, where her brother was working. Then took a look through the sweetie stalls on High Street and Reform Street with her. Came up to her Aunt's, Mrs Weir; stopped too long for the train and had to go down to Monifieth with her. A most beautiful moonlight night, which with the public lights here I was admiring coming home, where I arrived between 2 and 3 o'clock, but must be excused as it is the Fair day.

SAT. 27. My landlady went away to Glasgow this morning and is to stay till Monday night, so I will have to be my own cook till then, which is a job I don't like. Wrought tonight till 12 o'clock.

SUN. 28. Lay in my bed this morning, to my shame I must say, till 9 o'clock and then made some breakfast, of which I must say I made a very bad job. Went to Wallacetown Church, felt somewhat drowsy during the sermon, which was on the whole not over well fitted to arouse a drowsy hearer and was as short as it was dry; the whole service lasted only an hour and ten minutes. I then went and took a walk in the Baxter Park, where I sat for a long time and admired the beautiful view of the Tay and the adjoining coast of Fife. As I felt a little fatigued after last night's work I did not go to church again. Read a few psalms in the Park, came home between 3 and 4 and spent the rest of the night in reading. A sort of loneliness has come over me once or twice during the course of the evening and I could not keep from thinking that if I had a home of my own and a true friend with whom I could share my joys and sorrows that I would live much happier than I can do in lodgings, but I don't see things so clear before me yet to justify me in taking that step and the object of my choice does not feel herself at liberty either to give me her hand as yet, so we must put our trust in God, who knoweth what is best for us all, that he will provide all things for us in their right time and place. As I have to be at my work again at 12 o'clock I have not gone to bed at all.

MON. 29. Never stopped work till 9 o'clock on the morning of the 30th.

TUES. 30. Got the rest of the day to myself. Went down the town about midday and took a look round the harbour, then went to see the shows, which are here on the occasion of the Fair, and must say I was disgusted at the appearance of some of them outside and I suppose the inside was no better. There were machines there for telling you your weight, the force of blow that you could give an enemy, the strength of your wind and, as the exhibitors say, all the greatest wonders of the known world. One was exhibiting an extraordinary large ferret and rat and the only real gorilla alive in England. There were swinging boats and hobby horses in abundance and judging by the photographic salons one would think all the Dundonians have surely got a shadow of themselves now. I went over to Newport at 4 o'clock and took a walk down the water-side; was delighted with the view of the river from that side, which I think is far better than from Dundee. Came home between 7 and 8 and must say I was ready for my bed then.

WED. 31. Wrote a few lines of a letter to my brother George and brought forward this book which has been back for some nights.

SEPTEMBER

THUR. 1. Spent the evening in reading and writing.

FRI. 2. Had a visit of John Wright and spent the evening in interesting conversation with him.

SAT. 3. Got stopped work at 1 o'clock this afternoon to give us an opportunity of seeing the Prince and Princess of Wales who embarked here this afternoon for Denmark. Got a good sight of them as they passed along Dock Street, especially of the Prince whom I would easily have recognised by the portraits which I have seen of him. Went out to the Kellas after the procession was over, from thence to my father's at Panmure Monument.

SUN. 4. Came in by way of Kellas on Sunday night and got a short conversation with Anne Sturrock but could have taken one I don't know how much longer. Got company the rest of the way with J. Wright and got home about 9 o'clock.

MON. 5. Wrought till 12 o'clock at Scott's, Perth Road.

TUES. 6. Called on John Gibson at Mrs McHardy's.

WED. 7. Called on John Wright and spent the evening with him.

THURS. 8. Was along at Mr Crockett's, ironmonger, where I happened to meet Mary and Ann Findlay. Went along with Mary to her residence, Airlie Place, where I spent the evening.

FRI. 9. Wrote and went to the Post Office with a letter to Anne Sturrock, Kellas. Then read about an hour and a half at Walter Scott's *Poems*. It is now half twelve o'clock.

SAT. 10. Went down to the railway station to meet my brother George whom I was expecting. Waited for him till I thought he was not coming. Came up and took a walk in the Baxter Park, where a flower show was being held to celebrate the anniversary of the opening. Met my brother about half eight and afterwards went through the principal streets of the town with him, also the Watt Museum, and got home between 10 and 11.

SUN. 11. Got up at six o'clock and went to the top of the Law with my brother, where we got a most delightful view of the surrounding country. Went to Mr Ewing's church, then took a walk along the promenade at the shore. Then went through the Baxter Park and the Eastern Necropolis with him. Got some tea and went out with him the length of Claypots Castle. Went up to Baldovie Toll and along to Midmill. Waited a while for J. Wright and read a chapter or two of Ecclesiastes and was particularly struck with some of the verses. Got home about half past nine, read a while and went to bed.

MON. 12. Got a letter tonight from my cousin, Andrew Sturrock, with which I was particularly pleased. Was at a meeting in Lamb's Hotel, which was held for the purpose of instituting a Young Men's Christian Association for the town of Dundee. Got an account of the origin of the first society from a Mr Harris of London, who has been connected with them from the beginning, and some illustrations of the many benefits which have accrued from them in other large towns. A committee was formed to call a larger meeting on an early night when the society will be instituted, which I hope will meet with all success which it most richly deserves. However it is now half past twelve and I must haste to bed.

TUES. 13. Spent the evening alone in reading.

WED. 14. Went and joined the Watt Institution Library along with J. Wright and Alex Robertson. Took McClintock's *Researches after Sir John Franklin*. Took a stroll along the Nethergate after leaving the library and got home about ten o'clock.

THURS. 15. Wrought till eight o'clock, read a short time at McClintock and got to bed.

FRI. 16. Wrought till eight o'clock, then went along with J. Wright and spent about an hour with the Miss Packmans.

SAT. 17. Stopped work at two o'clock, then spent some time in showing my sisters, Ann, Isabella and Mary, through the town. Came up to Mrs Arthur's and got tea, then left for Monifieth with the quarter to six train. Stopped a short time at our sister's, South Grange, and arrived at the Monument about half past eight.

SUN. 18. Went to church in the forenoon. Started for Dundee about five o'clock. Came by way of the Kellas, where I met Elizabeth Packman, who came home with me, where we arrived about half past eight.

MON. 19. Wrought till eight, then spent the rest of the evening in reading McClintock's *Researches*.

TUES. 20. Wrought till eight, then read a while at the newspapers and McClintock.

WED. 21. Do. 10 o'clock.

THURS. 22. Do.

FRI. 23. Do. Received a letter from my father informing me that my brother George went to Aberdeen on Wednesday morning and listed with the 98th Highlanders and that he has sent word to them not to seek after him as he will not leave them, and as he listed once before and was bought off, it will be best to let him get his heart's content of them now. The shock which it has given my dear mother I am afraid will be too much for her.

SAT. 24. Got stopped work at two o'clock, then went along to Rodger's and stood for my carte de visite. Then took the train to Monifieth on my way to the Monument. Found my mother a good deal troubled about my brother's absence, but on the whole not so bad as I thought she would be.

SUN. 25. Came home on Sunday afternoon by way of Monifieth with my brother-in-law, William Hendry, and thence along the Ferry Road. Got a very bad night as it rained almost the whole of the road. Went along to the Post Office with a letter to my brother from my father and got Home about nine o'clock. Saw in an American newspaper at my father's on Saturday night of the death of one of my cousins in America from fever contracted in the army before Petersburg. He had a brother who fell before Richmond about a twelve months ago. They were both young men in the prime of life and their deaths must be a very sore bereavement to their family.

MON. 26. Wrought till 10 o'clock again.

TUES. 27. Do.

WED. 28. Got through with my late working last night at which I was very glad for I was heartily tired of it, in addition to it being a pretty stiff job which we were at, caging a heavy flywheel, which draws the sap out of one pretty well. Went in the town on some small errands after tea and read a short time at McClintock before going to bed.

THURS. 29. Spent the evening at home without doing anything in particular.

FRI. 30. Went along to Mr Rodger's for my cartes de visite with which I must say I am pretty well pleased. Then went to the library to exchange my book and got a treatise on the marine engine. Got home about eight o'clock, took a look at my book and read a while at the newspapers before going to bed. Got a letter from my father yesterday informing me that they had a letter from George and that he was heartily tired of the soldiers already and wishing he was off which we are to try to accomplish.

OCTOBER

SAT. 1. Got a full hour to breakfast today which we are henceforth to get without any reduction of pay and also all the rest of the foundries in town. Stopped work at two o'clock, went along and took a walk up the Baxter Park, then in the town, where I was half expecting to see Anne Sturrock. Looked about where I thought there would be any chance of seeing her but alas! she was not to be seen, at which I was somewhat disappointed. Came home to tea about six o'clock and bought the *Sunday Magazine* as I came up, a new publication by Dr Guthrie. Then wrote a letter to Anne Sturrock expressing my disappointment at not seeing her and setting a night when I would be out to see her. Spent the rest of the evening in reading the *Sunday Magazine* and newspapers.

SUN. 2. Got up about seven o'clock and took a walk in the Baxter Park before breakfast. Went to Mr Ewing's church in the forenoon, Mr McGaveny's in the afternoon and went and heard Mr Gilfillan's monthly lecture in the evening. Also finished the reading of my *Sunday Magazine*. Went along the town a bit with J. Wright about nine o'clock and got to bed between ten and eleven.

MON. 3. Went along with my fellow lodger, Mungo Smith, to Free St Andrews, Mr Ewing's church, to take a seat, but found that the meeting was postponed till tomorrow night. Went down for a short time to a sale of books in Reform Street. Got home between eight and nine, then brought forward this book which was back for some nights and now must get to bed, for it is eleven o'clock.

TUES. 4. Started to the Kellas after I got my tea, but by a stupid blunder of my own in not spelling Tuesday right, I was disappointed. I spelt it 'Thues' . . . which caused Anne to mistake it for Thursday, although she has told me since then that she read it over and over again to assure herself that she was right. As I deserved, I got a cold stand for my carelessness and had to trudge home again without getting anything to cheer me up, but not in the least angry with or blaming her at being disappointed.

WED. 5. Went along to Mrs Packman's where I spent an hour or two and spent the rest of the evening in reading.

THURS. 6. Did not get stopped work till half past two on the morning of Friday, 7 October, and as I had to be off early again I did not go to bed at all. Started at a quarter to five along with James Sturrock, Kellas, who occupied my bed all night, for the farm of Dryburgh to fire and attend to a portable engine and threshing machine. Got home about seven o'clock, then went along to the foundry about eight to get some orders from my foreman but did not see him. Was not long home when my manager's wife came along with them, and also Elizabeth Packman with whom I went along to her mother's and stopped till ten o'clock.

SAT. 8. Out at Dryburgh again. Did not get through till half past six. Got home at eight, dressed myself and went out to the Kellas with James Sturrock, where we arrived about half past ten.

SUN. 9. Did not get up till about nine o'clock, then went to church and had a sermon from Mr Boyd on the vanity of seeking true happiness in any other thing than serving God. Took a walk with Anne Sturrock after dinner with whom I spent the most of the afternoon very happily. Came home with J. Wright where I arrived between eight and nine.

MON. 10. Went along to my manager's, Mr John Sturrock's, house with a message from the Kellas. Came home about nine, then wrote a letter to the Rev. Mr Leslie, Arbroath, asking him to send me my certificate of church membership, then brought forward this book and got to bed about twelve o'clock.

TUES. 11. Went along to Airlie Place and put a lock on Mary Findlay's chest, where I stopped till ten o'clock.

WED. 12. Wrought till ten o'clock.

THURS. 13. Do.

FRI. 14. Do.

SAT. 15. Got stopped work at two o'clock then went out to my father's where I arrived about six o'clock (took the train to Monifieth).

SUN. 16. Did not get up till nine o'clock which I must say is a very bad way of spending the Sabbath morning and as I had a rather severe cold and a somewhat troublesome cough I did not go to church at all. Got home about eight o'clock, went in the town a bit with J. Wright and got to bed about eleven o'clock; but on the whole cannot say it was a well-spent day.

MON. 17. Went along after tea and met J. Wright at the Seminaries where we were intending to join an evening class for drawing, but owing I suppose to there being services in the churches tonight, it being Thanksgiving Monday, there was no class. We then strolled about a while through the town, went into Mathers' Coffee House and had a pie and ginger beer and had a look at the newspapers. I also bought a large cravat to put on in mornings and evenings as they are getting somewhat cold now. Got home a little before ten and now spent about an hour in writing.

TUES. 18. Spent the greater part of the evening in reading the newspapers, the bi-weekly *Advertiser*, which I sent off next morning to my uncle in America.

WED. 19. Got a commencement at the drawing school tonight. The hours of attendance are from half past seven to half past nine every alternate night for three months, fees six shillings, which is hardly twopence a night.

THURS. 20. Was intending to go out to the Kellas to see my Anne tonight but had to work till nine o'clock at which I was not very well pleased. But found when I came home a letter from Anne telling me not to come tonight which was a little consoling as I then knew I had neither disappointed nor kept her waiting.

FRI. 21. Wrought till nine o'clock again.

SAT. 22. Had to work till six o'clock. Then spent the rest of the evening at the fire-side reading. I was intending to have gone and seen Anne tonight but the weather said no, for it has poured down rain the whole day from morning to evening as long as I saw it. So we must console ourselves the best we can for a few nights longer.

SUN. 23. Got up about eight o'clock and as it still continued to rain I did not take a walk before breakfast which I usually do. Went and heard the Rev. Mr Ewing in the forenoon and afternoon. Spent the morning and interval in reading Dr Guthrie's *Sunday Magazine*. Commenced to write a letter after tea to Anne, but was hardly commenced when J. Wright came in with whom I spent about two hours in conversation on different subjects, then finished my letter, read a chapter and went to bed between eleven and twelve.

MON. 24. Wrought till ten o'clock.

TUES. 25. Do.

WED. 26. Wrought till nine o'clock.

THURS. 27. Got off at six, then went along to Mrs McHardy's to see John Gibson, where I stopped till ten o'clock, then took two hours at the drawing.

FRI. 28. Wrought till ten o'clock.

SAT. 29. Got off at two o'clock. Did not go out till seven. Spent the afternoon at the newspapers and doing small jobs at the tailoring business. Oh for one, I need not say who, to do them for me! Stopped about an hour and a half in the town and spent the rest of the evening in reading and drawing till almost twelve o'clock.

SUN. 30. Got up a little before eight. Went to the Baxter Park before breakfast. Then went and heard Mr Ewing in the forenoon. Went out the length of Stobs Toll between the services with J. Wright, and I, hurrying back to go to church, who should I meet coming along the street here but my Anne who being in the town today had been calling on me when I was out. I was most agreeably surprised at seeing her and as my landlady and bedfellow were both away at church I brought her in here for a short time. We then went along to Mrs Packman's as her brother George and Miss Dykes were there. They started about five o'clock for home. I went out to Stobswell with them. I also got her carte de visite from her tonight. Spent the rest of the evening in reading, except a while's conversation with J. Wright.

MON. 31. Wrought all night.

NOVEMBER

TUES. 1.11.64. Went to the library with my book and did some other small errands coming home, where I arrived a little past eight and as I was somewhat tired after last night's work I was not long in going to bed.

WED. 2. Wrought till eight, but cannot say I then did anything before going to bed.

THURS. 3. Wrought till eight, then had a while's writing before going to bed.

FRI. 4. Wrought till eight and then had a while at the drawing.

SAT. 5. Got stopped at two o'clock, then went out to my father's.

SUN. 6. Did not get up till about nine o'clock. Went to church in the forenoon and started at five o'clock to come home. Came in by the Kellas and got an opportunity to chat a while with Anne. Came in with J. Wright and Margaret Packman. Went along to her mother and stopped a while and got home about ten o'clock. Got a newspaper at my father's today from an old sweetheart now married in New Zealand.

MON. 7. Eight o'clock again and expect to be so all the week. Spent the rest of the evening in reading the New Zealand news.

TUES. 8. Eight o'clock again, then sat down to have a while at the news but slept the most of the time. I may also say that this is my birthday which makes me twenty four years of age. How time flies! It seems little more than a few weeks since I remember telling some of my playmates that I was nine years old! And was proud of it too, thought I was something then. Alas! Poor mortals! We are all rather prone to think we are something more than what we actually are.

WED. 9. Eight o'clock again. Then wrote, and went to the Post Office with, a letter to James Keay, a millwright with whom I am acquaint, giving him from my foreman an offer of a job at Lilybank Foundry.

THURS. 10. Got off at six o'clock tonight and then spent the evening at Mrs Packman's in company with the Misses Packman and a few acquaintances in some little amusements on the occasion of Hallowe' en.

FRI. 11. Got off at six o'clock and as this is one of the nights that the drawing class meets I ought to have been there, but as my landlady and fellow lodger had a number of their friends and acquaintances invited tonight to have a little sport on the occasion of Hallowe' en, I could not with propriety go away. We had a first rate evening's amusement which we kept up till between one and two o'clock. We then, to the number of five couples, went out to the Baxter Park and had a reel in the Pavilion. Came back and separated at the end of Victoria Street. I had to go along to Barrack Street with a Miss Anderson, a milliner, and got home at three o'clock.

SAT. 12. Got through at two o'clock. Then went out with Elizabeth Packman to the Kellas where there was also a little sport on the occasion of Hallowe'en, which is tonight. We broke up between ten and eleven. I spent an hour most happily with Anne. It is most delightful to have a true and loving friend with whom one can spend an hour now and then. It helps to drive away the cares and troubles of our daily life and seems a foretaste of that happiness which I yet hope to enjoy with one I dearly love, I need not say who.

SUN. 13. Did not get up, to my shame I must say, till past nine o'clock. Went and heard the Rev. Mr Boyd from whom we got a good sermon on Mary choosing the one thing needful. Alas! How few of us even think of that one thing while we are blessed with health and strength. Spent the most of the afternoon in chatting with Anne and Elizabeth Packman. We got a somewhat wet and dirty night to come home in. Stopped a short time at Mrs Packman's and got home a little before ten o'clock.

MON. 14. Wrought till ten o'clock. Then took a while at this book bringing it up. My bed-fellow and I had also a pretty long discussion on the virtues and qualities which a good wife ought to possess. We are both of opinion that we would be much better of a good wife, but neither of us will have one in a hurry for all that I think. But all things considered I intend to have one as soon as possible to. Got to bed at one o'clock.

TUES. 15. Wrought till ten o'clock. Then had a little more writing and got to bed at twelve o'clock.

WED. 16. Got stopped at six and got to the drawing class for the first time since I joined it on the 19th October. Then brought forward my time book in which I am keeping a note of what I am working at and also the extra time that I work and the time I am paid for.

THURS. 17. Wrote and went to the Post Office with a letter to J. Wright who met with a rather sad accident on Friday the 11th. His foot was caught and the toes nearly torn away by the eccentric of a steam engine that he was working at. He was taken out to his father's the same day and I have been very careless in not sending a few lines ere this time to enquire for him, neither going myself to see him, especially as I was at the Kellas which is within ten minutes' travel of his father's. Cleaned my drawing tools after I came home and did some other little nicknacks and got to bed about eleven o'clock.

FRI. 18. Got to the drawing class again. Then wrote a little before going to bed about twelve o'clock. Received a most welcome letter tonight from one of my cousins in America, Barbara Sturrock, in which she was telling me of the death of one her brothers, who was in the army, after suffering eight weeks from fever contracted in the camp before Petersburg. He is the second brother who has lost his life since the commencement of the war. I also got a note from my father telling me that my brother George, who listed some time ago, got home on Saturday and that William, who has not been very well for some time, is not like to get much better yet, poor fellow.

SAT. 19. Got off at two o'clock, then took the train to Monifieth on my way to see my brother James at Buddon Stables, with whom I stopped all night.

SUN. 20. Got up about eight o'clock, then came along about midday, to see my sister Clementina where I stopped all afternoon. Left at six o'clock to come home. Called on Margaret Wright as I came past but she happened to be out. Got home about eight o'clock and to bed at half past ten.

MON. 21. Wrought in the shop till ten o'clock after working till six at Schelesman's factory, Pole Park, putting up shafting at cogwheel for him after six. Took a look at the papers after I came home and got to bed at twelve o'clock.

TUES. 22. At cogwheel again till ten o'clock, then took a while at the pen. Got to bed at twelve.

WED. 23. Do. Wrought till five o'clock in the morning.

THURS. 24. Do. Wrought till ten o'clock.

FRI. 25. Got off at six and very glad of it. Then wrote, and went to the Post Office with a letter to Anne and took a while at this book, bringing it up before going to bed.

SAT. 26. A quarter to three till I got off tonight. Then went out to my father's at Panmure Monument.

SUN. 27. Did not get up till about nine o'clock again. Went

to church in the afternoon. Then went along to my brother David's at Panmure Cottages after dinner, where I got my tea. Came home by the Kellas as usual, where Anne was anxiously awaiting my coming. Had a while's conversation with her, then went in and had a talk with her father who, I think, is beginning to be aware of my intentions towards his daughter. I was afraid for some time that he would be opposed to our union but am beginning to change my mind now and would fain hope that things will turn out to be all that we could desire yet. Came in by James Wright's and found that John's foot was almost whole again. Got home at half past nine and got a very dark wet stormy night to come home in. It was a heavy rain the whole way from Kellas to Dundee.

MON. 28. Wrought till past ten at Schelesman's factory.

TUES. 29. Do. till ten.

WED. 30. Do. Very tired tonight heaving up shafting and putting it in its place.

DECEMBER

THURS. 1. Wrought till twelve o'clock tonight to get started tomorrow.

FRI. 2. Got started to-day when all went off pretty well. Got off at six, which is a sort of about now, and spent the evening in filling up my books which were both back for more than a week.

SAT. 3. Did not get off till a quarter past three. Then went in the town and bought some articles of clothing. A fancy woollen shirt, flannel for ditto, and a new coat. Came home to tea between six and seven. Took a look at the newspapers and went in the town again for my coat as I had not money with me the last time to pay for it. Came home a little past nine. Sat down to the newspapers and did not get to bed till almost twelve o'clock.

SUN. 4. Did not get up till nine o'clock again, a very bad habit, which I am getting into which I must try and shake off. Went and heard Mr Ewing forenoon and afternoon but felt drowsy and listless at both services. Took a walk down to the shore, along the promenade and out the Nethergate a bit between the services. My bed-fellow had a Mr and Mrs McLean, friends of his, at tea with him tonight with whom I spent a while in conversation. I then went along to hear Miss Armstrong, the lady preacher, in the Corn Exchange but cannot say what sort of a sermon it was as I could not hear, but by what I did hear and see I think she is a first class speaker. J. Wright came in tonight to commence work tomorrow as his foot has got pretty right again. Read a while at the *Sunday Magazine* before going to bed about eleven o'clock.

MON. 5. Got to the drawing tonight, then wrote a little before going to bed between eleven and twelve which is my general bed-time.

TUES. 6. Wrote a letter to my cousin Andrew Sturrock, gardener at Skelmorlie Castle near Greenock.

WED. 7. Got to the drawing again. Then wrote a little after coming home.

THURS. 8. Went along to the Scouringburn to see J. Wright and I found that he had not been able to be at his work all day from a disordered stomach and a sore head. But he was better then and thinking to go to his work next morning. Had a letter from my father today in which he was telling me that my brother William had got another son and also that my eldest brother, Alexander, had been laid up with a rheumatic fever some days since, which I earnestly hope he may easily get over. I may also state that I bought a small locket tonight in which I intend to give my portrait to Anne as a New Year's present.

FRI. 9. At the drawing class tonight.

SAT. 10. Went along to Mr Rodger's after dinner, intending to stand for my portrait, but it was too dull and dark for it tonight. Went down to the shore and took a look through the shipping. Came up through the fish market and got home about five o'clock, then spent the rest of the evening at the fireside in reading the newspapers and writing part of the letter being a few lines for Anne. Got to bed about eleven o'clock.

SUN. 11. Got up at half past eight. Went to Mr Ewing's church in the forenoon, Mr Adamson's, Wallacetown, in the afternoon, who I must say is in my opinion a dry preacher. I was intending to go and hear Miss Armstrong in the evening but was prevented by J. Wright coming in, as we must always have an hour or two's conversation when we get the opportunity. We had almost two hours tonight on two or three different subjects. I then went and hear Mr McGregor of Free St Peter's, who delivered a sermon in Mr Bewick's chapel, Bell Street, on behalf of the newly formed Young Men's Christian Association. He gave a most eloquent and impressive sermon on Romans 14, 7 and 8: 'For no man liveth to himself and no man dieth to himself. For whether we live, we live unto the Lord; and whether we die, we die unto the Lord.' It would be well for us if we would keep those words more in mind than we do but alas! our guilty hearts will think of nothing but this world and its vanities.

MON. 12. At the drawing class tonight.

TUES. 13. Spent the evening at home in reading and writing.

WED. 14. At the drawing class again.

THURS. 15. Went on the town and bought some little articles. Came home between eight and nine. Then took a turning about among my clothes and spent the rest of the evening in arranging them and the other stuff in my chest.

FRI. 16. Wrought all night at the foundry putting up shafting for connecting, also the new engine for driving the work, also all Saturday the 17th, till twelve o'clock at night. My sister Ann who was in town came up when I was at my dinner, expecting to get me home with her, and as I thought I might get off at six o'clock, she stopped till then for me and as I could not get away, she stopped all night with Mrs McHardy.

SUN. 18. Got up at half past eight, got some breakfast and went along to Mrs McHardy's but found they were only new up. Left for the Monument with my sister at half past ten and arrived at one o'clock. They were all there but my oldest brother, Alexander, has been laid up for two weeks past with rheumatic fever and is no better yet. Came home by the Kellas and had a while's conversation with Anne, and arrived home in company with J. Wright a little past nine.

MON. 19. My brother-in-law William Benny from Monifieth, came in when I was at my tea, asking if I had seen Ann on Saturday, as she had been stopping with them for some days before and was intending to go back on Saturday night when she left them, as my brother George, who was seeing them on Sunday, said she was not at the Monument on Saturday night, they were afraid that she had done, what she once did before, run away. But happily I was able to give them evidence to the contrary. I then went down to the Station with him and thence along to Mr Rodger's. Came home and sat down to have a while at the newspapers, but soon fell asleep as I was somewhat tired after so much work on Friday and Saturday and travelling on Sunday.

TUES. 20. Went along to the Packman's with J. Wright, where we spent the evening.

WED. 21. Spent the evening at home in bringing forward my journals.

THURS. 22. Spent the evening at home in drawing.

FRI. 23. Was at a supper tonight in the Albion Hotel with some fellow workmen, the manager and all the foremen connected with the engine work on the occasion of these engines starting, where we spent a very agreeable evening till 11 o'clock.

SAT. 24. Went down to the public baths after dinner and had a warm bath and a cold shower, which I think I will be a great deal better of. Then bought some trifles and came home to tea or rather I should say coffee which I prefer to tea about six o'clock. Got a pair of everyday boots tonight also with which I am very well pleased both in appearance and price, which is thirteen shillings and sixpence. Spent the evening after six o'clock at home in writing a letter to Anne and reading the newspapers.

SUN. 25. Got up at eight o'clock and took a walk the length of the Eastern Necropolis before breakfast. Went to St Mary's Roman Catholic chapel this afternoon in which it being Christmas Day solemn high mass was performed at noon, which in my opinion is a piece of the merest trumpery that ever I saw. I could not help wondering to myself when the priests were going through their ceremonies and manoeuvres if they actually believed such ceremonies were acceptable to God. For myself I must say I was little other than disgusted with them. Went home and heard Mr Ewing in the afternoon and felt somehow or other that I was home again, or at least more where I should be, when I got in Free St Andrews. Got an excellent sermon from Mr Ewing, which he closed with the words, 'Go to Christ now this very night. Tomorrow may be too late.' Most solemn words certainly if we could only keep them in our mind, but alas! the depravity of our hearts will not allow us to think of words so much to the point as these. Spent the evening after tea at home principally in reading.

MON. 26. Went along to the drawing school but found there was no class tonight. Got home again about eight and spent the most part of the evening at the needle, doing some small jobs at the tailoring business.

TUES. 27. Spent the evening at home and did nothing in particular except giving a walking stick which I am finishing for my brother David a rub of sandpaper.

WED. 28. Went along to Mrs McHardy's expecting to see her son Patrick who is over from Liverpool seeing her at present. But he happened to be out so I did not see him. Came home about ten o'clock.

THURS. 29. Wrought till eight o'clock, and as I was intending to have gone out to the Kellas to see Anne tonight, I wrote a letter to her after I got home telling her the reason I could not get out tonight.

FRI. 30. Had to work all night.

SAT. 31. Had to work till twelve o'clock at night. Another year is now past. Another measure of time is gone. Gone forever beyond our reach and whether we have improved it or trifled it away there is now no remedy. Oh! that we would keep this in mind more than we do. It would keep us from doing many a thing which we afterwards wish we had never done. Grant O God that we may keep it more in mind in the present than we have done in the year that is now past.

1865

JANUARY

SUN. 1. Slept this morning till half past ten and being still somewhat tired and also four or five inches of snow on the ground I did not go to church today. I was not in fact beyond the door the whole day. Spent the most part of it in reading the *Sunday Magazine* but was like to take a nap sometimes. Got my tea in company with a few friends of my landlady's with whom I spent two hours or so very pleasantly. Had also a short chat with J. Wright and went to bed at half past eight, as I had to be at my work at twelve o'clock again.

MON. 2. Had to work till eleven o'clock tonight.

TUES. 3. Wrought all night.

WED. 4. Got through with my extra work at this time at six o'clock this morning and very happy at it. I now intend to have the rest of the week to myself and have a little enjoyment also on the occasion of Auld Yule which I intend to spend at home among my friends. To begin with I called on Mrs McHardy after breakfast time and then went in the town and bought some trifles and took a look about me for some time, as there was not a train to Monifieth till ten minutes to one. Called on my sister Clementina at the South Grange and got home to my father at five o'clock and as I was both tired and sleepy by that time I went to my bed about seven and lay till a quarter to nine next morning.

THUR. 5. Yule Day. Went along in the forenoon to my brother David's at Panmure and then to Alexander's at Guildy who I am sorry to say has been laid up with a rheumatic fever for five weeks now and little or no prospect of him getting any better yet. Went back to the Monument again and started for the Kellas at three o'clock, where I arrived about half five, and got my tea with Anne and her father with whom I spent part of the evening most happily. Then went up with Anne and her brother James and his wife to their home where we spent another two or three hours most delightfully and got to bed about twelve o'clock.

FRI. 6. Spent the whole forenoon one way or another here and started at twelve for my brother William's at Greystone, Carmyllie. Called on David Sturrock at Lucieslap [sic] as I passed, where I got dinner. Then on to his brother Alexander and his mother who was my apprentice mistress and a good one I must say she was to me. I was very kindly treated by them all and invited back again to see them. Arrived at my brother's at five o'clock, who I am sorry to say is nothing better yet, but I don't think he is any worse either. Got my tea with him and his wife from Peter Cameron, his next door neighbour. Then called on my aunt Margaret and her husband, James Murray, who I am sorry to say has had a slight stroke of paralysis which has disfigured his face a little. Otherwise they are both quite well.

SAT. 7. Stopped here till midday then started for my father's.

Spoke in to Mrs Lumgair's on my way south and also my
brother Alexander who is nothing better yet. Called and paid
John Spalding, tailor, for some clothes making and got home
a little before dark about as tired as though I had been working
hard all the week. Attempted to read once or twice in the
course of the evening but it always ended in a sleep. Went
to bed between ten and eleven.

SUN. 8. Got up about eight o'clock. Went to church and heard
a good sermon from Mr McIntyre although to my shame I must
say that tonight, Wednesday, I remember little or nothing about
it. Started at half past four for Dundee. Came by the Kellas and
had a while's conversation with William Sturrock and Anne,
and then of course a while by ourselves. Got home about nine
o'clock somewhat tired as the roads were very bad tonight. Got
to bed about eleven.

MON. 9. Got commenced to work again this morning as
usual. Was intending to have spent this evening at home,
but J. Wright came in about eight o'clock, with whom I went
along to Mrs Packman's where we stopped till half past ten.
Went along to the Cowgate with him. Took half an hour at
the pen when I came home and got to bed at twelve o'clock.

TUES. 10. Went in the town for some trifles but mainly for a
locket and portrait from Mr Rodger's, with which I must say I
am highly pleased. Went up to Mrs McHardy's, when I came
home (as I got a locked door here) and had a crack with John
Gibson. Came home at ten o'clock, took a while at the pen
and got to bed between eleven and twelve, my usual time.

WED. 11. Had a whole evening writing, bringing up this
book.

THURS. 12. Spent the evening in reading and writing.

FRI. 13. Finished, and went along to the letter box with a
letter which I commenced at dinner time for Anne telling her
that I could not be out tomorrow night as I intended, as I
have to go to Dunblane tomorrow morning. Trifled away the
rest of the evening and did nothing in particular.

SAT. 14. Started this morning at ten minutes to eight for
Dunblane, where I arrived about half past ten, to do some
repairs on the shafting of Alex. Wilson and Co's woollen mill.
Commenced at two o'clock and wrought till twelve.

SUN. 15. Lay in bed till half past nine, then started between ten and eleven to see the Wallace Monument, which is about four miles from Dunblane. Passed through the Bridge of Allan which is a most beautiful and romantic little village consisting almost entirely of a first class style of houses fitted up for the convenience of summer visitors, of which it receives an immense number during the summer months. The Monument is situated about two miles south-east of Stirling on a bold lofty eminence known as the Abbey Craig. It is built in a bold warlike-looking style, very strong and altogether well worthy of its object. It is about 150 ft high at present and is to be 200 when finished. It will be a noble monument for a noble man. We went into a hotel at the foot of the Craig when we came down to get some refreshment which appeared to be a regular drinking shop on Sunday. There were three sitting drinking in the room to which we were shown with whose conversation I was perfectly disgusted. As we were within two miles of Stirling we then took a walk that length and got a look through the castle which is a fine strong ancient building, the west side of which is situated on the very brink of what I would call an inaccessible precipice. There is a most beautiful little cemetery adjoining the Castle which we next took a look of. I think it is one of the most beautiful spots that ever I saw. It is very rocky and romantic and adorned with some noble monuments and statues. Most prominent among the former stands the Martyrs' Monument erected in memory of those who shed their blood for their religion and their liberty. Among the latter are John Knox and several other noble Scotchmen. There is a most beautiful view got from the cemetery as well as the Castle, in which one of the most conspicuous objects is the beautiful River Forth winding in numberless sweeps and curves which it is hardly possible to trace on its south-eastward course towards the ocean. We then went round the Castle Hill which is skirted the whole way round with a nice walk, which is a favourite walk with the good folks of Stirling, crossed the bridge which spans the Forth and turned our faces homewards, where we arrived at seven o'clock, for myself well-pleased with what I had seen but not so well with such a manner of spending the Sabbath, which to say the least of it is far from right. As we had to be at our work again by twelve we got to bed about eight.

MON. 16. Wrought till midnight again.

TUES. 17. Wrought till half past two in the morning.

WED. 18. Got finished about breakfast time, then packed up our tools and took them to the station and as we did not get a train till ten minutes to two, we went up and got a sight of the ancient cathedral, which of itself is worth going a bit to see. It is about seven hundred and fifty years since it was founded and most of it is still in a pretty good state of preservation. There is a small part of it roofed in and used as the parish church. Of the rest there desolation. We arrived home here in Dundee about five o'clock very cold and somewhat hungry, and kept pretty close to the fireside after I got down to it. In fact I slept the most part of the evening at it. Got to bed about ten o'clock.

THURS. 19. Spent the evening at the pen bringing forward this book.

FRI. 20. Went out to the Kellas tonight to see Anne with whom I spent part of the evening very happily. Got home a little past twelve o'clock.

SAT. 21. Had to work till twelve o'clock tonight fastening cogs in the flywheels of our foundry engine.

SUN. 22. Lay in bed till nine o'clock and was not outside of the door till I left for church at eleven o'clock. Went down to take a walk along the Marine Parade after service, where I met David Findlay and William Macdonald who had come in from the Kellas to get a sight of the town and as neither of them knew much about it I did not go to the church in the afternoon but went through the principal parts of the town with them, the Baxter Park included. We then came and got some tea and went along to Mrs Packman's, where we stopped till about seven o'clock when they set out for the Kellas and I came home to my lodgings and as I had to be back to the cogs fastening again by twelve o'clock I went to my bed a little past eight. Was all morning to six o'clock at the cogs.

MON. 23. Spent the evening at my pen filling up my books.

TUES. 24. Went to the town tonight and bought two hats, one for my father and another for my brother William, and then took a look about me for a while and got home a little before nine and finished up and varnished a walking stick for my brother David before going to bed.

WED. 25. Spent the most part of the evening at Mrs McHardy's.

THURS. 26. Spent the evening at home in reading and writing.

FRI. 27. Trifled away the evening at two or three things without doing anything in particular.

SAT. 28. Got off at two o'clock tonight, dressed myself and went along to Mrs Packman's, where Anne and her sister-in-law, Mrs James Sturrock, were waiting me, with whom I went out to the Kellas and from thence to the Monument where I arrived a little past eight and found them all in the enjoyment of good health. My brother Alexander is also getting better again.

SUN. 29. Lay in bed till nine o'clock again. Really I am getting very lazy on Sunday mornings but I must make an effort and shake it off again, for I am not at all pleased with myself for lying so long on Sabbath mornings. Heard an excellent sermon from Mr McIntyre on the words: 'Great is our Lord and of great power. His understanding is infinite'. He closed with the solemn admonition to call upon the Lord while he is to be found, for that time was with all short and uncertain and might with some of us be closed this very night, words which we all know to be true but which we will not act upon as if they were true. Came home by way of the Kellas and had of course a crack with Anne and got home about half past ten.

MON. 30. Read a while at the newspapers, wrote a little and had a while's conversation with my fellow lodger.

TUES. 31. Not being very well tonight I went to bed about seven o'clock and did not go to my work till ten next morning.

FEBRUARY

WED. 1. Went in the town a while tonight. Got home at half past eight, took a look at the *Sunday Magazine*, which I bought, wrote a little and got to bed about ten, about an hour earlier than usual.

THURS. 2. Spent the evening at the fireside without doing anything except reading a short time at Walter Scott's *Poems*.

FRI. 3. Slept a good part of the evening at the fireside and read a little at Scott's *Poems*.

SAT. 4. Spent the afternoon at the newspapers. Went in the town at half past six and got home again a little past eight. Then wrote a little and read a little at Scott's *Poems* before going to bed.

SUN. 5. Lay till nine o'clock as usual and went to Free St Andrews in the forenoon and afternoon. Happened to see an old acquaintance, Bythinia Emers, at church in the forenoon, with whom I went along the Nethergate a bit. Went and heard the Rev. George Gilgillan's monthly lecture in the evening on the religious aspect of Ireland. Got home about eight o'clock and read a while at the *Sunday Magazine* before going to bed.

MON. 6. Working till ten o'clock tonight and will be for all the week.

TUES. 7. Do.

WED. 8. Do.

THURS. 9. Do.

FRI. 10. Do.

SAT. 11. Got off at two o'clock and spent the afternoon at the newspapers. Then went in the town and happened to meet Elizabeth Packman, with whom I went along to her mother's and stopped till about ten o'clock. Then took a look at Crabbe's *Poems* which I bought tonight and also a Valentine for somebody. Got to bed about twelve o'clock.

SUN. 12. Got up at half past eight, half an hour earlier than usual. Went to Free St Andrews forenoon and afternoon, and heard a sermon in the evening by the Rev. Dr McGavin on behalf of the Young Men's Christian Association on 'Young Men – their Obligations and Blessings', and which the Rev. Doctor handled in a very eloquent and impressive manner. Happened to meet Helen Wright as I was coming home, with whom I turned and went a short way in the Nethergate. Got home a little before nine. Read a chapter and psalm and went to bed about ten.

MON. 13. Working till ten o'clock.

TUES. 14. Took this evening to myself and went to the Scottish Reformation Society's annual festival or soiree, where I enjoyed myself nicely and was so highly pleased with the proceedings and object of the society that I intend to join it the first opportunity. Got home about eleven o'clock.

WED. 15. Working till ten again.

THURS. 16. Do.

FRI. 17. Do.

SAT. 18. Got off at two o'clock and then went out to my father's. Took the train to Monifieth and got a very coarse night to go up in, as it was a heavy snow almost the whole way and also three or four inches lying on the ground.

SUN. 19. Got up at half past eight and found it a fearful day of snow and drift which continued the whole day with little or no intermission, in consequence of which I did not get to church and had given up hopes of getting in to Dundee either. But it faired up about five o'clock and I started and got not such a bad night as I expected I would have got. Came in by the Kellas as usual where I stopped about an hour and a half and of course had two or three minutes of a crack with Anne. Got home at ten o'clock.

MON. 20. Working till ten o'clock again.

TUES. 21. Do.

WED. 22. Do.

THURS. 23. Do.

FRI. 24. Do.

SAT. 25. Got through at two o'clock and took a while at the newspapers after dinner. Then dressed and went down and had a look at the shipping in the harbour, then up and down a short time in the town and home to tea about six. Then took a look at the *Sunday Magazine* which I bought and went in the town again a little before eight and stopped about an hour and a half, wandering about here and there, having nothing to do in particular. Went up the Overgate and came down again and don't think I was ever so disgusted with it as I was tonight, for what with the smell of spirits and tobacco I thought I would have been choked before I got out of it and thought that I actually breathed more freely when I got upon the High Street again. Took a look at the newspapers again after I got home and went to bed a little before twelve.

SUN. 26. Got up at eight o'clock and intended having a walk before breakfast, but being a wet morning I did not go out. Went and heard Mr Ewing as usual forenoon and afternoon. Had a walk along the Marine Parade before coming home between the services. Went out after tea and had a walk round the Baxter Park in company with my bed-fellow. Was called in to J. Sturrock's as we were coming back, so went in and had a while's conversation with his mother, who was my apprentice mistress, about the changes that had been taking place about Luckyslap since I left it. Got home about eight o'clock and found Margaret Wright here with whom I went up to Stobswell. Was home between nine and ten, read a chapter and psalm, and got to bed between ten and eleven.

MON. 27. Got through at six o'clock tonight and hope to do so all the week. Was intending to have a whole evening's writing, but a young lass, Catherine Goodwin, who stops directly above us and with whom we often have a while's conversation, we spent the evening till nine o'clock in conversation and amusement. We then went up with her to her father's to get a sight of her library of which she has a pretty good one, out of which I selected Dick's *Christian Philosopher* to have a read of in exchange for some of mine which she has been reading. Had of course a crack with her father and mother also, who were both very frank and friendly with us and appear to be a very well-living happy family indeed and one whose acquaintance I will be most happy to cultivate. But I must go to bed now, for it is past one o'clock and I have been scrawling away at the pen since a little before eleven.

TUES. 28. Wrote a letter to my cousin Andrew Sturrock. My bed-fellow and I then sat and chatted together till almost 12 o'clock.

MARCH

WED. I. Wrote a letter to my cousin Thomas Petrie and then one to Anne and did not get to bed till almost one o'clock.

THURS. 2. Was along at Mrs McHardy's and her daughter Mrs Arthur's tonight. Came home a little before ten and had almost half an hour's writing or so before going to bed.

FRI. 3. Wrote a letter to my cousin Barbara Sturrock in America.

SAT. 4. Got off at two o'clock. Took a while at the newspapers after dinner and then went in the town and looked about me a while and went and had a warm bath at the public baths, which I really think I am the better of. Came home to tea a little past six, spent a while more at the newspapers and some other trifles and then wrote a letter to my brother William at Carmyllie and did not get to bed till almost twelve o'clock.

SUN. 5. Got up about eight and was intending to have a walk before breakfast but it happened to be a wet morning and I did not go out. Went and heard Mr Ewing as usual in the forenoon. My bed-fellow and I then took a walk along the Marine Parade, then up and along the Nethergate and out the Perth Road a bit till church time as we were going to hear Mr McGregor of St Peters, from whom we got an excellent sermon from the words, 'Go ye into all the world and preach the Gospel unto every creature', the duty of which he pointed out in a very striking and forcible manner. Met Helen Wright when I came out with whom I went along to the east end of the Magdalen Green where she is residing at present. Went along after tea and heard the last of George Gilfillan's course of lectures on Ireland, which in my opinion he has handled in a very able and masterly manner. Got home about eight and had a while's reading before going to bed about eleven.

MON. 6. Went out to the Kellas tonight to see somebody . . .

TUES. 7. Went in the town on some errands tonight. Got home at nine and did some writing before going to bed.

WED. 8. Got one of my eyes hurt today with a chip of metal, so much so that I can hardly open it at all especially in gaslight, so went to bed between seven and eight.

THURS. 9. Went to my work in the morning as usual but found it would not do, as I could not bear the light on my eye at all, so did not go back after breakfast time. Got a shade made to keep the light out of it and went along to Blackie and Son's office in the Nethergate with Scott's Bible to get bound for my sister Ann. Then went down to have a look at the shipping in the harbour, but found I could not look upon the water at all, so held along to the very east end of East Dock Street, up to the Ferry Road, went out a bit, then up to the Baxter Park and stopped in it till about two o'clock. Set out again about half past four and went out to the West Mains, then down the den and came in the toll road, and got home about six o'clock, and as I could not manage to read any I was not very long in getting to bed again.

FRI. 10. Went to my work again today but was very bad at looking upon anything on which the sun was shining or which was of a light colour. Went down to the High Street in the evening for my dress hat which I was getting altered. Was home about eight o'clock and had then a while's conversation with my bed-fellow and a friend of his which was calling on him. Tried to write before going to bed but could not look so long upon the paper as I could write a complete word.

SAT. 11. Got off at two o'clock and went out to my father's. Took the train to Monifieth as usual and then got company to the Craigton with an old school-fellow, James Sheriff, a pattern maker in the East Foundry.

SUN. 12. Got up about eight o'clock and took a walk round the top of the hill before breakfast time. Went to church as usual and started for Dundee at half past six. Did not get an opportunity for a crack with Anne at all tonight, as Elizabeth Packman and Ann Findlay were both there, with whom I got company in. Went down to the Shore Terrace with Ann Findlay where we arrived exactly at ten o'clock. Got home and got to bed about eleven.

MON. 13. Went along to the Post Office Savings Bank but found it shut, so just turned and came home again and took a while at this book, filling up, which was back for three or four days. Then wrote a letter to J. Wright, who is at present in Brechin. Did not get to bed till almost twelve o'clock.

TUES. 14. Working till ten o'clock again.

WED. 15. Do.

THURS. 16. Wrought all night.

FRI. 17. Wrought till eight o'clock and got to bed by nine.

SAT. 18. Took a while at the newspapers after dinner. Went in the town a while and was home again by half past five. Went down again a little after seven and put some money in the bank. Stopped about an hour. Took a look at the newspapers again and did some writing before going to bed.

SUN. 19. Got up about half past seven but did not go out to have a walk before breakfast as it was a cold stormy morning with occasional showers of hail, which had continued the whole day. I accordingly took the nearest church in the forenoon – Mr Skene's Free Wallacetown – Mr McDougall's Chapelshade in the afternoon, and heard Mr McGregor in the evening who delivered a sermon in St Paul's on behalf of the National Bible Society, whose claims on public support he laid down in a very striking and forcible manner. Got home a little past eight and sat down to read, but somehow or other I could not put my thoughts upon reading, so I gave it up and gave scope to them and then had a while's conversation with my bed-fellow after he came in and got to bed at eleven o'clock.

MON. 20. Went in the town and got my hair cut. Was home again a little past eight and did some writing and some other little trifles before going to bed.

TUES. 21. Wrote a few lines of a letter to Anne which I finished and went along to the letter box with by eight o'clock. Then employed myself till about ten o'clock in drawing a sketch of a vertical boring machine which I saw at Dunblane when I was there, which for simplicity and convenience is the best I have seen yet.

WED. 22. Went out to the Kellas to see my Anne tonight with whom I spent about two hours most delightfully. Started to come home about ten or a little past it and was overtaken by a cab about half roads and got a drive the rest of the way. Arrived at eleven o'clock but trifled about a while and also read some bits of Milton's *Paradise Lost* and did not get to bed till twelve.

THURS. 23. Went and saw Professor Pepper's Ghost or rather Ghosts tonight, which I think is one of the most wonderful and curious contrivances which ever I saw. You could almost swear sometimes that it was real living persons jumping and dancing about on the stage and appearing and disappearing you could not tell how, and in proof that they were shadows and not real persons you can see a real person through them and also one ghost through another. It is really one of the most perplexing exhibitions that ever I saw. Got home at ten o'clock, did some writing and did not get to bed till about twelve.

FRI. 24. Spent the evening in drawing a sketch of a vertical boring machine or at least trying to do so.

SAT. 25. Took a while at the newspapers after dinner and did not go out till after tea which I took about five o'clock. Went down and took a walk round the docks, came up and got some things I was in need of, and was home again by seven, and was just set down to have a quiet evening by myself at the fireside when James Sturrock, Kellas, came in and being on his way home he would have me to start with and bear him company which I accordingly did without much entreaty. We first went along to Mrs Packman's and stopped a while and got out to the Kellas a little past ten.

SUN. 26. Lay in bed till half past nine o'clock and being a cold spring day with some snow on the ground and occasional fierce showers of it I did not go far from the fireside till church time, when I went down and heard Mr Boyd, getting a seat as I always do when I got there with Anne and her father. Went down with James in the afternoon and spent two hours or so with them, where we all got our tea together, his wife and family being all there too. Started to come home about seven o'clock and was expecting to get J. Wright in with me, he having got home from Brechin on Thursday, but found him in bed with a bowel complaint which seized him on Saturday morning and with which he had been in bed all Sunday. Got home a little before half past ten and got to bed a little past it.

MON. 27. Took a while at my journal, filling up, a look at the newspapers and did some other little things.

TUES. 28. Had a while's conversation with my bed-fellow after tea and spent the rest of the evening in reading *Dick's Christian Philosopher*.

WED. 29. Spent the evening in practising my hand at drawing.

THURS. 30. Read at the *Sunday Magazine* for April the most part of the evening.

FRI. 31. Did a little at the drawing tonight but trifled away about an hour after tea without doing anything.

APRIL

SAT. 1. Got a rise of one shilling on my wages today which was perfectly unexpected. Got through at two and met my brother George as I was coming home, who was in search of a job, having got tired of the place he was at in the country. So after getting some dinner and dressing myself we set out to see if we could find one and happened to be successful at the second shop we tried. We then left per railway for Monifieth about half five and arrived at the Monument a little past six o'clock.

SUN. 2. Did not get up till nine o'clock. Went out and had a walk round the wood and through the walks till almost church time. Took a look through the greenhouses in the afternoon and trifled through the rest as I generally do there without hardly reading a word. Started about five as usual to come in and got plenty of company after I came to the Kellas, as Eleanor and Margaret Packman, George Milne, and Mr and Mrs John Sturrock were all there, with whom I came in and landed about half past eight o'clock. Read a chapter and psalm and got to bed a little past ten.

MON. 3. Had about an hour's conversation on religion with my bed-fellow. After tea went along to Mrs McHardy's and stopped till ten o'clock with John Gibson, then started to my journal and books, filling up, and must now haste to bed for it is about half twelve o'clock.

TUES. 4. Went along to a sale of furniture in the Corn Exchange Hall but not seeing the article I was in quest of, I did not stop above ten minutes of quarter of an hour, but went along and called on J. Wright, with whom I stopped till ten o'clock.

WED. 5. Had a good while's conversation with my bed-fellow after tea, then varnished the stock of his rifle for him, he being a member of the Highland Company of Volunteers. Then read a while before going to bed at a book entitled *'Is It Possible To Make The Best Of Both Worlds'*.

THURS. 6. Dressed myself after tea with the intention of going out, as I was expecting J. Wright along, when we were going to call on Mrs and the Misses Packman. But as he did not come I spent the evening at the fireside professing to be reading Dick's *Christian Philosopher*, but I rather think that Morpheus (sleep) came in for the best share of my attentions.

FRI. 7. Lounged about a good while after tea without doing anything, then took a while at the *Advertiser* which I bought today, containing the particulars of the opening and some of the trials in the Circuit Court which opened here yesterday, being the first ever held in Dundee and of course creating quite a sensation in the town. Then addressed the paper for my uncle in America and did some other writing before going to bed.

SAT. 8. Off at two o'clock as usual and was dressing myself in all haste expecting my brother George in with his trunks when he came in but no Trunks with him as he could not get a horse and cart today, they being all so busily engaged with the seed putting in at this season of the year. So we then went down the town and looked about a while, had a look at the shipping in the harbour and then went east to the new or Camperdown Dock and was taking some refreshment in Dock Street Refreshment Rooms previous to his leaving with the quarter to six train when he remembered that I had not shown him where his lodgings were, which I had got for him during the week, and consequently he would not know where to go with his trunks if he happened to get them in on Monday. So we came up to Mrs McHardy's, she having got them for me, who took us across to them, they being just a little east of her a few doors up Victoria Street in Victoria Square. He then went down to catch the ten minutes to seven train, and I went along and had a walk through the Baxter Park. Was home a little before eight, read a while at the newspapers and scratched down the afternoon's transactions before going to bed about eleven o'clock as usual.

SUN. 9. Got up at twenty minutes past six and took a walk down the river to the Stannergate and as it was a perfectly beautiful morning it was a perfect treat to get out and enjoy the pure fresh air of the river-side. Was home again a little past eight and took a look at the *Sunday Magazine* till church time. Went and heard Mr McDougall of Free Chapelshade in the morning and Mr Knight, Free St Enoch's, in the afternoon. Happened to meet Helen Kydd, an old acquaintance, and her two fellow servants between the services, with whom I went along to their residence in the Nethergate and stopped till almost church time in the afternoon. Went and took a walk in the Baxter Park after tea and took a seat at the foot of the flagstaff for a good while from which I admired the beauties of the park and the surrounding scenery. Met Elizabeth Packman as I was coming out of the South Gate on my way down to church again, with whom I turned and went out and had a walk through the New Burying Ground and went up and stopped about an hour in her mother's on my way home where I arrived about eight and had a while's reading before going to bed about half past ten.

MON. 10. Was just set down and had got one line of a letter written to Anne when my brother George, who has got his trunks in today, came in and in a few minutes also J. Wright on his way to call on the Miss Packmans whose father, Captain Packman, who has been absent almost two years, came home today. We then went along together and stopped till half past ten, after which I finished my letter to Anne and got to bed at twelve o'clock.

TUES. 11. Wrought till twelve o'clock tonight at J. Gordon's engine.

WED. 12. Was intending to have gone out to see Anne tonight but had to work till half past six and as it takes me almost half an hour to come home, I had just to content myself without seeing her tonight and did nothing except filling up my journal, before going to bed, which was back for two or three days.

THURS. 13. Wrought till ten o'clock.

FRI. 14. Do. all night.

SAT. 15. Got through at two o'clock and spent the afternoon till six o'clock in sleeping and reading the newspapers alternately, then went out after tea and took a walk through the Baxter Park and was home again by half past seven and wrote a few lines to Anne telling her the reason that I could not get out to see her on neither Wednesday nor Friday night as I intended. Then took a while at my books, filling up, and got to bed about half ten o'clock.

SUN. 16. Got up at a quarter to eight and went out and had a walk in the Baxter Park before breakfast. Then got ready and went along to Free St Peter's Church today and also my brother George, where we heard an excellent sermon from Mr McGeorge on Hebrews 9, verses 16 and 17, 'For where a testament is, must also of necessity be the death of the testator. For a testament is of force after men are dead; otherwise it is of no strength at all while the testator liveth'. He divided it into three heads: I the testator, II the testament and III the legatees, and enlarged at considerable length on each in succession. The Rev. William Arnot from Edinburgh who was assisting him in serving the tables, it being the sacrament today, gave some very beautiful addresses also. We stopped till the conclusion of the services at a quarter past four and so interesting were they that I did not weary in the least. I went in the evening to Free Wallacetown and heard one Dr Gibson from Glasgow, who gave an excellent discourse from the words, 'Who loved us and gave himself for us'. I then went out the road a bit to meet John Wright in company with his sister Margaret and my landlady and as usual went in the town a bit with him and got home a little before ten.

MON. 17. Went out to the Kellas tonight to see Anne, with whom I spent about an hour and a half most delightfully. We then went in to her brother James where I stopped another hour fully and did not get home till half past twelve.

TUES. 18. Read till half past seven at today's *Advertiser*, then washed myself, and addressed and went down to the Post Office with it for my father to let him see the particulars of the fall of Petersburg and Richmond which is contained in today's paper. I then sat down to write a little after I got home and was intending to get to bed soon tonight, but I got into a conversation about love, and the time slipped past with us till it was past eleven before we got to bed.

WED. 19. Trifled away the evening till eight o'clock without doing anything except going down Princes Street for some lotion for my eyes, having got one of them hurt with a chip of metal. I then did some writing, bathed my eye and got to bed about half past nine.

THURS. 20. Took a walk down to the harbour tonight where I met my brother with whom I took a look at the shipping for a while. Then came up the town and bought some small articles. Happened to meet J. Wright and stopped a short time with him and got home about half past nine. Got a locked door when I came home and to put off the time took a step along to the east end of the street where I met Helen Wright on her way home, who asked me if I would go along with her, which I did as she had a pretty long road to go, no less than to the very west end of the Magdalen Green. Met my bed-fellow coming up the edge of the Green as we were going down, who had been along seeing his sweetheart who stops somewhere down there about. He turned back with us and we then came home together, where we arrived a little past eleven o'clock.

FRI. 21. Went down to Dens Brae top of Princes Street to see an old friend and bed-fellow, John McKinnes, who got married about a month ago to Miss Jessie Dandy with whom I was also acquainted. I spent a very happy evening with them and did not get home till a little past ten. I then did a little writing and did not get to bed till half past eleven.

SAT. 22. Got through at two o'clock and spending about an

hour looking about the town in company with my brother we left with the half past four train for Monifieth. George Milne and Eleanor and Margaret Packman went down with the same train with whom we got company up to the Monument, or at least almost, for although they were within a hundred yards of my father's house, there would none of them go in with me.

SUN. 23. Did not get up till a little past eight and only had a short walk round the wood before breakfast. Went and heard Mr McGregor as usual and started at five o'clock for Dundee. Stopped a short time at the Kellas and also at James Wright's, and got home at a quarter past nine, in company with J. Wright and one James Croll who was out seeing James Sturrock at the Kellas. Did not get a conversation, nothing like what I would have liked, with Anne tonight. Had a nice opportunity too, if only my brother had been a bit out of the way.

MON. 24. Took a while at the newspapers after tea and then tried a little practice at arithmetic, and in proof of the general saying that perseverance is always rewarded I managed to do a rule in vulgar fractions with which I have been beat two or three times before. I then took a while at my books, filling up, and got to bed a little past eleven.

TUES. 25. Spent the evening at home in reading a while at Templeton's *Millwright's and Engineer's Companion*, and a while at Dick's *Christian Philosopher*. Got to bed about half past ten.

WED. 26. Went down to Reform Street and put some money in the Savings Bank for my brother Robert. Met James Hendry in the Bank and went down to the High Street with him, where we were joined by J. Wright and had a while's conversation together. J. Wright and I then went down to the harbour and thence along to the Camperdown Dock and looked about a bit and back to the High Street again. Got home at ten o'clock and was informed by my landlady that she was to try and do without lodgers any longer and consequently that I would have to leave on Saturday week, which I must say gave me more pleasure than pain as I have been thinking of trying a change for some time past.

THURS. 27. Took half an hour or so at the *Advertiser* after tea, which I bought today to get the particulars of the assassination of President Lincoln and Secretary Seward of America which arrived yesterday forenoon and with which I must say I was horror struck, an assassin being in general looked upon as a mean dastardly coward and having chosen for his time the very hour of victory it makes the act if possible more horrible and heart rending. I then went out and spent a while in the Baxter Park with J. Wright. Was back here again by nine o'clock and had an hour's conversation together before he went away. Got to bed about eleven o'clock.

FRI. 28. Went along with my bed-fellow to Mrs Arthur's and stopped a few minutes. Then went across the street to enquire about lodgings, but found there was only an opening for one and as we would like in together again if possible, that of course was not to our mind. We then went in the town and went down and had a walk round the docks. Came up and gave Mrs McHardy a call and got home at ten o'clock.

SAT. 29. Set out after dinner in company with my bed-fellow in search of lodgings which we succeeded in getting down in Princes Street after a little searching about. They are not just exactly what we would have liked but they will do for a time and we can take the first opportunity of better ones which turns up. We then took a turn through the Baxter Park, went in the town and looked about us for a while till tea time. Went in the town again at seven o'clock, went down and had a look at the shipping in the docks and wandered about a while without going anywhere or doing anything in particular except going in to the shoemaker's for a pair of boots on my way home, where I arrived about a quarter or twenty minutes to nine o'clock. Then had a while at the newspapers and also a nap of a sleep and being somewhat tired as well as sleepy I got to bed at half past ten.

SUN. 30. Got up at six o'clock and went out to the Den of Mains to enjoy the fresh morning air for a while. It was a most beautiful morning and I was highly pleased with my walk so much so that I did not get back again till a little before nine. I went along and heard Mr Knight in the Thirle Hall in the forenoon, and happening to meet James Hendry as I was taking a walk at the shore between the services, I had a while's conversation with him and then went along with him to Free St Paul's in the afternoon and heard Mr Borwick in the evening, who delivered a very able sermon in St James's

U.P. Church, the late Mr Reston's, who was taken ill in the pulpit last Sabbath and expired in about an hour. I then went out the road and met J. Wright and went in the town a bit with him and met his sister Margaret and Ann Findlay with whom we stopped a quarter of an hour or so. I then came up with his sister and got home a little before ten.

MAY

MON. 1. Had to work till eight o'clock tonight and then wrote and went down to the Post Office with a letter to Anne.

TUES. 2. Was preparing to have a while at my journal, filling up, when David Findlay, who has commenced work to-day in town with Baxter Brothers, came in and in a little after, my brother George and from one thing to another the evening passed over till it was ten o'clock till they left. I then commenced to my writing and did not go to bed till twelve o'clock. Received a letter today from my cousin Barbara Sturrock in America in which she mentioned the downfall of Richmond and great rejoicings in the North in consequence. Judging from her words Northerners must have a most bitter hatred at Southerners or Rebels as they always call them. She calls Richmond the home of the vilest traitors that ever polluted this earth. I also received a portrait of her oldest brother Andrew with which I am highly pleased.

WED. 3. Went along to see J. Wright and then started together for a walk out the Blackness Road. Went out a mile and a half or two miles then down to the Perth Road, came in a bit, down to the Magdalen Green, came in that way in the Nethergate and up to the top of the Murraygate where we separated a little before ten. Had a while's writing after I came home and did not get to bed till twelve o'clock.

THURS. 4. Spent the evening at home doing sundry little nick nacks such as arranging my clothes and books, etc., previous to removing and read a while at Dick's *Christian Philosopher* before going to bed at half past eleven.

FRI. 5. Had to work till eight o'clock. Then did some trifles and took a while at the *Christian Philosopher* before going to bed at half past eleven. Had a letter from my Anne tonight in which she told me that she intended to be in Broughty Ferry tomorrow afternoon and would be very happy to see me there if it was convenient for me to get down, she being aware that I have to remove tomorrow night.

SAT. 6. Got my clothes and things all packed and made ready for removing and then went in the town with my bed-fellow and got a cart to remove our chests. Was about half past four till we got removed which made me too late to get down to the Ferry in time to see Anne which I intended to have done if we had got removed in time. I then took a look at the newspapers till tea was ready, after which I went up with my bed-fellow to the Barracks to see the Volunteers drilling and then wandered about the town up and down here and there till eight o'clock by which time I was perfectly weary of it. I then went down to the Corn Exchange Hall to see a Diorama of Jerusalem, the Holy Land, Syria and other eastern views, with which I was highly pleased. Got home a little before ten and was not very long in going to bed.

SUN. 7. Got up at a quarter to seven and went out to the Baxter Park where I enjoyed myself most delightfully till about nine, admiring the various flowers and shrubs who are all beginning to get green and beautiful now. Went and heard Mr McDougall today. Took my usual walk along the Marine Parade and sat down a while till church time and then went up and heard Mr McGregor who of all the ministers I have yet heard in town is the one I like best. Took a while at the *Sunday Magazine* after tea and then went along to hear Mr Gilfillan, but found when I got down that instead of going in to the church they were coming out of it, it was that full. I then went up to the Corn Exchange to hear John Bowes who was to be on the same subject, namely, the fall of Richmond and the assassination of President Lincoln, which subject he handled in my opinion in the most miserable manner that ever I heard any subject handled in, so much so that great numbers, and myself among them, left before he was near finished. Got home a little before eight, had an hour's writing and a while at the Sunday Magazine before going to bed about half past ten.

MON. 8. Dressed myself and took a look at the newspapers till half past seven and then went along to Mr McGregor's Bible Class to which I was invited by Helen Wright and with which I was very highly pleased. I also spoke for a seat tonight but have very little hopes of getting one, there has been such a demand for them before now. Got home at ten o'clock, had a while's writing and got to bed about half past eleven.

TUES. 9. Spent almost the whole evening in conversation with my bed-fellow on two or three subjects and then read a short time at the *Christian Philosopher* before going to bed at half past ten.

WED. 10. Working till ten o'clock.

THURS. 11. Do.

FRI. 12. Do.

SAT. 13. Got off as usual at two o'clock, dressed myself and went in the town and looked about me a while and then started with the half past four train for Monifieth and arrived at the Monument in company with my brother about a quarter past six.

SUN. 14. Did not get up till a quarter to nine. Went and heard Mr McIntyre as usual and started at five o'clock for Dundee. Stopped a while at the Kellas as usual and got two or three minutes' conversation with Anne, but not half so much as I would have liked. I have not got a quiet crack with her for a long time now and beginning to weary for another opportunity of spending an hour or two in company with my own dear Anne. Came along by J. Wright's as usual. Stopped a short time there and got home a little before ten.

MON. 15. Went along by J. Wright's and then went down together to St Peters, intending to go to Mr McGregor's Bible Class, but found that there was none tonight, he being away from home some way. We then took a walk out the Perth Road for a mile or so, went down and crossed the railway to the river side and came along that way to the Magdalen Green. Came in the side of it, which is a most delightful walk now that the trees and flowers are beginning to get green and beautiful. Came in the Nethergate and up to the restaurant in Reform Street and had a pie and ginger beer and got home at ten o'clock. Took a while at my books, filling up, and did not get to bed till almost twelve o'clock. Well pleased as yet with my new lodgings and think I will be far more comfortable here than where I was before.

TUES. 16. Went in the town and bought a large pot for my sister Clementina and some little articles for myself and was home again by eight o'clock and then wrote a letter to my darling Anne.

WED. 17. Wrought till ten o'clock.

THURS. 18. Do.

FRI. 19. Wrought all night.

SAT. 20. Got through at five o'clock. Looked a while at the newspapers after dinner and was on my way in the town about four o'clock when I met my brother Robert whom I was expecting in the forenoon and had now given up hopes of seeing him tonight, and more than that, who should he have in company with him but Miss Allan, teacher at Greystone, Carmyllie, who has been in town for a day or two at present, seeing her father and mother who reside here and who had been down at the station waiting him. I then turned with them and went up to her father's in Church Street, where we stopped a while, and then went out to the Baxter Park together, where we stopped till half past seven, and after getting some tea, we went up to her father's again for her, when she told us she had been getting a scolding for not taking us along with her to get tea. I then went down to the station with them and saw them off on the train for Carnoustie. I was expecting my brother to have stopped with me all night but as she had to be home to her school again on Monday morning and there being no trains on Sunday he of course could not let her go away herself. I then went up to the High Street after leaving the station and looked about me a while and got home at nine o'clock. Made an attempt to read the newspapers but found it wouldn't do, so got to bed a little before twelve.

SUN. 21. Lay in bed till half nine today and did not go out for a walk before breakfast but took a look at the *Sunday Magazine* till that time. Went up to Mr McPherson's church today but he did not happen to be preaching himself. Went down in company with my bed-fellow and took a walk along the Marine Parade which I generally do between services and went up and heard Mr Ewing with him in the afternoon. Took a while at the *Sunday Magazine* after tea and then went out to the Baxter Park. Took a seat up at the foot of the flagstaff and admired the beauties of the Park and the surrounding scenery for a long time. Went up and out through the new burying ground to Stobs Toll and thence out the road and met J. Wright and got home at half ten.

MON. 22. Spent the evening at home and at my books, filling up, and did not get to bed till half past eleven.

TUES. 23. Was along seeing the Diorama of the Holy Land again tonight in company with J. Wright and his sister Margaret who got a prize of a mahogany writing desk there. I went along with John and her to the Magdalen Green and carried home her desk for her and bought some paper and envelopes on the way out as a hansel to it. Got home at half past eleven.

WED. 24. Was out in the Baxter Park tonight with J. Wright and one of his fellow workmen where there was a great turn-out tonight, the Artillery Band being performing there on the occasion of its being the Queen's Birthday. We stopped till about half past nine and then went in the town and out the Nethergate to the Magdalen Green and back to the High Street where we separated. Got home at eleven o'clock.

THURS. 25. Trifled about without doing anything in particular till eight o'clock, when J. Wright came up when we went up to Mrs Packman's. Stopped till about half past nine then went in the town a bit with him and got home at ten o'clock.

FRI. 26. Having got a heavy load of cold somehow or other I was in no trim for reading or any other thing tonight, so sat at the window the whole evening looking out to see what was passing up and down the street.

SAT. 27. My sisters Ann and Mary being come to town today, I did not go to my work after nine o'clock, but dressed myself and went down to the High Street and met them at ten o'clock. I then went with them to get their portraits taken and spent the forenoon going about the town with them till a little past one when I brought them up to my lodgings to get some dinner. We then went up and called on Mrs Arthur and her mother, Mrs McHardy and left with the half past four train for Monifieth. Went up to our sister's at the South Grange where we got tea and stopped a while and got home a little before eight.

SUN. 28. Lay in bed till nine o'clock and being no better of my cold yet, I took a dose of physic before breakfast, so of course I could hardly go to church and being a wet sort of day, I sat in the house almost the whole forenoon and started for the Kellas a little past three where I got my tea with her father and brother and likewise got a short conversation with Anne. Had

a good long one with her brother George but would have been
as well pleased if I had got the long one with Anne with whom
I have not got a quiet crack for a long time now. Got home a
little before ten o'clock.

MON. 29. Being no better of my cold tonight but rather worse,
as it has sitten down into my breast today, so much so that I have
had a great difficulty in breathing, together with a hard hacking
cough, I went down to Dr Greig of the Dundee Laboratory who
gave me a powder to take among some gruel before going to
bed and also some castor oil to take in the morning and said
I would be much better to give up work for a day or so.

TUES. 30. Did not get up till about a quarter to nine today
and intend taking the rest of the day to myself also. I have
not been quite so bad for breath as I was yesterday but the
cough is still somewhat troublesome. I have spent the whole
day in the house, about as much from necessity as choice as
from shortness of breath and weakness together the slightest
exertion tired me. I have done little or nothing the whole
day but looked out at the window, except doing a little at
my journal, filling up, in the afternoon, which was back for
four or five days. Went to bed about half past nine.

WED. 31. Lay in bed till a little past eight and intend taking
the rest of this day to myself also. Am a great deal better today,
the cough being now the worst thing that is troubling me. Had
a pretty smart attack of it for a while after going to bed last
night. Went down between ten and eleven to Dr Greig's and
got a bottle of cough mixture, then down and had a look at the
shipping in the harbour and east to the Camperdown Dock and
had a look at it, and only got home a little before two o'clock.
Read a little and took a while at my journal, filling up, again
in the afternoon. Read a while at Dick's *Christian Philosopher*
after tea and went to bed a little before nine.

JUNE

THURS. 1. Commenced to my work this morning again but
have not got nearly rid of my cough yet, of which I had a
smart attack last night again. Went in the town tonight for my
sisters' cards with which I must say I am not particularly well
pleased. Was home again a little past eight and of course had

a good look at the cards then and read a while at the *Sunday Magazine*, which I bought tonight, before going to bed.

FRI. 2. Been a good deal better today. Spent a while in conversation with my brother, who was up tonight, and read a while at the *Sunday Magazine*. But in truth I have trifled away a good part of the evening without doing anything.

SAT. 3. Got off at two o'clock as usual, then cleaned and dressed myself in all haste to meet Anne who came in a little before two and whom I saw and spoke to as I was coming home from work. Went to Mr Rogers with her to get her portrait taken for carte de visite. Took a walk round the harbour and saw the Watt Museum, etc., etc., and walked about till half past six, when she started for home, accompanied of course by myself, who could not at the least leave her till she was the longest half of the way home at any rate. Stopped a short time at Mrs Packman's on the way out and instead of going part only, I went home with her altogether, and stopped with her brother James all night. We enjoyed a nice talk by ourselves on the way out, taking plenty of time and not hurrying ourselves in the least. Arrived at the Kellas a little past nine, had two or three minutes of a crack with her after that and did not get to bed till twelve o'clock.

SUN. 4. Lay in bed till half past eight and went to Hillock Free Church in the forenoon with James Sturrock. Had a walk with Anne in the afternoon with whom I spent about two hours or so very pleasantly. Then got tea with her and her father and brother George, and went down with them to Murroes Church, where there was a service tonight and is to be fortnightly during the summer. Mr McMurtrie of Mains or Tealing, I forget which, conducted the service tonight, with which I was well pleased. Started to come home about eight o'clock. Came in by J. Wright's with whom I got company in and arrived here at quarter to ten o'clock.

MON. 5. Went down to the High Street and got a bottle of cough mixture. Then went to the shore and had a warm bath which I enjoyed very much. Got home a little before nine and took a while at my books, filling up, before going to bed.

TUES. 6. Took a while at the newspapers after washing myself and went to bed at eight o'clock, and got a mustard plaster on my chest to try and relieve the cough which is not like to leave me very soon and has been settling down into my breast for some days past. Kept it on for an hour and twenty five minutes and could have kept it on longer not finding it near so painful as I expected it would have been from what I have heard of them, it being the first I ever had on, but perhaps it was not so strong as some of them are made.

WED. 7. Read a while at Dick's *Christian Philosopher* and took a while at my journal, filling up. Went to bed at half past nine and got another mustard blister tonight. Found it a good deal smarter than the one I had on last night. Don't know how long I kept it on.

THURS. 8. Found my breast very smart this morning when I got up – and has been a little the whole day, but I have been better today than I have been for a week past. Went along to Mr Rogers for some of my cards which I ordered on Saturday past but they are not to be ready till Saturday coming, Anne's only being ready, with which I am highly pleased. He has made a first class job of them I think. I then went along to J. Wright's where I only stopped a few minutes and came along to the Post Office with him. Went down to the harbour and had a look at the shipping. Took a walk along the Marine Parade, round the Camperdown Dock and up to the Cowgate where we separated at ten o'clock. Took a while at my books filling up after coming home and did not get to bed till fully half past eleven.

FRI. 9. Working till ten o'clock.

SAT. 10. Got off at two as usual and after dressing myself went in the town and along to Mr Rogers' for my cards which were to be ready tonight but were not. Met J. Wright on the High Street as I was waiting for my brother George. Went and had a drink of lemonade together and came up the length of the Cowgate with him and then down St Andrews Street to the station and left with the half past four train for Monifieth and arrived at the Monument a little past six.

SUN. 11. Lay in bed till half past eight. Went to church in the forenoon and was somewhat drowsy even after lying so long. Started at half past five for the Kellas where I stopped a good while and only got home at a quarter to ten.

MON. 12. Working till ten o'clock again. Took a while at my books, filling up, after coming home and did not get to bed till almost half past eleven.

TUES. 13. Went in the town on some errands and was home again about half past eight. Took a look at the newspapers, put some portraits into my album and altered and arranged the others, and took a short while at my books, filling up, before going to bed about eleven o'clock.

WED. 14. Working till ten o'clock.

THURS. 15. Do.

FRI. 16. Went in the town for my cartes de visite and some other little things. Then down to the harbour and looked about me a while, then east and round the Camperdown Dock, which is now finished and almost full of water and is to be opened in the course of a week or a fortnight. Got home about a quarter past nine and trifled about without doing anything in particular and did not get to bed till about eleven.

SAT. 17. Got off at one o'clock as usual. Took a look at the newspapers after dinner and did not get ready to go out till half past three, when I went in the town on some little errands then down to the Perth or Union Street Station to see about the Saturday excursion trains, next Saturday being our annual holiday, when I intend to take a trip to Pitlochry, to see the far famed Pass of Killiecrankie. Did not leave the station till fully five o'clock, there being a large party of excursionists from Carron leaving at the time I was there which I stopped and saw away. I then went by East Dock Street and the Ferry Road to the Stannergate, where I took a seat at the waterside and enjoyed myself very nicely for about two hours or so, having a beautiful view of the river and the opposite coast of Fife, besides taking an occasional look at the newspapers which I had with me. I then came in the Ferry Road again and down to the station, where I arrived just as the Volunteers were coming out from Monifieth, where there was a grand review of all the Volunteers in the county this afternoon by the Earl of Dalhousie, Colonel Jones (Inspector of Volunteers) and several others and which was finished up by a sham fight between the Artillery and Riflemen. Met my bed-fellow who is a member of one of the Highland Companies at the Station and took a stroll through the town for a while together and did not get home till a quarter past ten. Then took a while at my journal, filling up, and did not get to bed till almost twelve o'clock. Highly pleased with my afternoon's enjoyment.

SUN. 18. Got up about half past seven and had a walk in the Baxter Park before breakfast. Went up to Hilltown to hear Mr McPherson but was disappointed as he was not preaching. Nevertheless I heard an excellent sermon from the words, 'Simon! Simon! Satan hath desired to have thee that he may sift thee as wheat, but I have prayed for thee that thy faith fail not'. Came home after the sermon and took a look at the *Sunday Magazine* and went down in the afternoon to Chapelshade where I also heard an excellent sermon on the ten virgins, five of whom were wise and five foolish. Read a while at the *Sunday Magazine* after tea and went out between five and six to the Baxter Park with my bed-fellow where we sat and enjoyed ourselves for a good while and then went out to the Necropolis or New Burying Ground, which is a most beautiful place and took a walk through it also, and got home at a quarter to nine and took a look at the *Sunday Magazine* again. Read a chapter and psalm and got to bed at eleven o'clock.

MON. 19. Had a letter from J. Wright this morning who went away to Coupar Angus last Monday to put up two engines there. Went up to my shoemaker in Victoria Street to get some tackets put in my boots, but he happened to be out of the kind required so did not get it done. Called up to Mrs Arthur's and stopped a short time and was home again about eight. Then cleaned a spy-glass which I intend taking to Pitlochry with me on Saturday and did some other little trifles before getting to bed about eleven o'clock.

TUES. 20. Was all night fitting a cog-wheel along at North Tay Street.

WED. 21. Went out to the Kellas tonight to make some arrangements with Anne and her brother George who are going to Killiecrankie with me on Saturday. Got a good long crack with Anne who was particularly kind and delighted like with me tonight. Parted with her at half past eleven and got home at a quarter to one, pretty tired and sleepy too by that time.

THURS. 22. Working till ten o'clock.

FRI. 23. Went in the town for some little things and was home again by half past eight and took a while at my books, filling up, and laid out my clothes, etc., to be in readiness in the morning, tomorrow being our annual holiday at the Foundry

which I intend spending in company with my Anne, her brother
George, and Miss Dykes at Pitlochry and Killiecrankie. Got to
bed at half past ten.

SAT. 24. Got up a little before five, was dressed and had
breakfast by a quarter to six, and went out the road about
a mile and a half and met them coming in from the Kellas.
Got down to the station just in time for the seven o'clock train
to Perth and got a compartment of a second class carriage to
ourselves, so we had a very comfortable journey up to Perth
and enjoyed ourselves nicely. Arrived there at eight o'clock and
looked about us a while and got some refreshment before the
train started for Pitlochry at half past nine. Had to take second
class tickets at Perth as there were no third issued with that
train. Arrived at Pitlochry at a quarter to eleven. Of the village
itself I can say nothing as we did not go through it but held
directly out the toll road to the famous Pass of Killiecrankie,
which is about three or four miles north from Pitlochry and
through which both the railway and the toll road passes. I will
not attempt to give anything like a description of the scenery
either of the Pass or of the route up from Perth, but merely
say that from Dunkeld especially all the way to Killiecrankie
it is to the lover of the wild and romantic in nature very
beautiful and interesting. We went up the toll road between
two and three miles and then went down to a nice walk in
the bottom of the Pass which goes up the whole length of it
to the top. We did not go far up when we sat down and took
some refreshment and enjoyed ourselves for a good while on
the banks of the Tummel, which comes down the Pass and
whose waters are here particularly clear and beautiful. Anne
and I then set out together and went up to the top of the
Pass and in my opinion were well repaid for our trouble, for
the view which we got there was really one of surpassing beauty
and grandeur. We then went up about a mile further with the
intention of seeing the old battlefield, but we happened to be
on the wrong side of the water having crossed it on a bridge
down at the top of the Pass. We were both highly delighted
with our walk having gone up very leisurely and taken plenty
of time to look about us. When we came down again to where
we left George and Miss Dykes we found that they were away.
They came up to the top of the Pass a while after us but not

finding us there, they got wearied waiting and set out on their
way down to Pitlochry again and were about half an hour or
so before us. The train left here for Perth at ten minutes to
six and the second class carriages being full, we got into a first
class one and had a very comfortable seat down to Perth, where
we arrived a little past seven and in Dundee at twenty minutes
to nine and being somewhat hungry by that time we went to
the coffee house in Dock Street and had a cup of coffee and
steak, and then went along to the Arbroath Station and took
the last train for Broughty Ferry which did not get away till
ten o'clock tonight, a quarter of an hour behind her time. We
then took a cab from there to the Kellas where we arrived at
ten minutes past eleven, all of us highly pleased with our day's
enjoyment. Got to bed at twelve o'clock.

SUN. 25. Got up at half past seven and after getting breakfast
with Anne and her father, having stopped with them all night
for the first time, always stopping with her brother James before,
any night that I happened to stay at the Kellas. I went down
to the Murroes Church with them and Mary Findlay who was
at James Sturrock's today. Went up and stopped a while at
James's after dinner, and then went down again with Anne
and Mary Findlay and spent the afternoon with them till tea
time, after which I spent an hour very *pleasantly* with Anne and
started to come home about seven o'clock, Mary Findlay being
away about half an hour or so by that time, which I purposely
stopped for, not wishing to put myself in the way of her and
her sweetheart, who was out meeting her, enjoying themselves.
Got home at a quarter to nine and met up with Mary and her
sweetheart at the end of the Lilybank Road and came down
Princes Street to my lodgings with them.

MON. 26. Spent the evening at the newspapers and my books,
filling up, and went to bed about eleven o'clock.

TUES. 27. Went along to Constitution Road where Margaret
Wright is now stopping with Mr Kydd, builder, and spent
the evening with her till ten o'clock. Started to my journal,
filling up again, after I came home, and did not get to bed
till a quarter to twelve.

WED. 28. Went up to my shoemaker in Victoria Road
and got some tackets put into my boots. Had a while
at my journal, filling up again, after I came home and

read a while at Dick's *Christian Philosopher* before going
to bed.

THURS. 29. Went to see Sanger's Circus tonight, where there
was an immense number of spectators, as it is to be only a few
days in the town. It is well worth going to see for one night but
after that it has no interest for me. Got home at ten o'clock.

FRI. 30. Spent the evening writing a letter to my cousin
Andrew Sturrock.

JULY

SAT. I. Had to work this afternoon and did not get home
till about a quarter past nine. Was along at James Irons' Mill
putting on two cogwheels and a very dirty job it was. I then
wrote a few lines of a letter to my father after I came home,
as I was intending to have gone out tonight and they were
expecting me and would be wondering what had come over
me if I had not sent them a few lines to let them know I was
working.

SUN. 2. Got up about half past seven and went out and had
a walk in the Baxter Park before breakfast. It is looking very
beautiful at present, there being a rich blossom of flowers now.
I take great pleasure in having a quiet walk through it on Sabbath
morning which I generally have every Sabbath that I am in the
town. Went and heard Mr McPherson today and being their
quarterly Sacrament there was no interval in the middle of the
day, so I stopped till the tables were all served which was at
four o'clock. Took a look at the *Sunday Magazine* after tea and
went along to Chapelshade Church where I heard an excellent
sermon and also a long one for we were no less than two hours
and twenty five minutes in the church. Saw Margaret Wright
as I was coming home and stopped a quarter of an hour or so
with her. Got home a little past nine and went to bed about
half past ten.

MON. 3. Trifled about a while after tea without doing anything
and then wrote a letter to John Wright who is at present in
Coupar Angus and a pretty long one I gave him too and did
not get to bed till almost twelve o'clock.

TUES. 4. Got a letter from my cousin, Andrew Sturrock, this
morning, from whom I have not heard for six months before,

and would not yet had I not sent one to him on Saturday giving him a blowing up and telling him that since he had got married he was like to forget all his old friends and acquaintances now. It seems he had lost my address which was the reason he gave for not having written to me sooner, but the letter also contained the news that he is now the happy father of a little daughter. So of course he is to be excused if he is like to forget some of his old friends now. Went in the town tonight and was home again by half past eight. Then read a while at the *Sunday Magazine* which I bought and took a while at my journal, filling up, before going to bed at half past eleven.

WED. 5. Spent the evening at home and wrote a letter to Anne and to my cousin Andrew Sturrock of Craigton, Monikie, who has got a situation with the Water Company in town here and having promised to try and get lodgings for him I succeeded this morning in getting accommodation for him with an old acquaintance of his own, Ebenezer Arklay, in Victoria Street. Got to bed about half past eleven.

THURS. 6. Went in the town tonight and looked about me a while, then down to the harbour and had a look at the shipping and east to the Camperdown Dock and looked at them a while, drawing out the piles of the coffer dam, which is a very slow and laborious process. Got home about half past nine and took a while at my journal, filling up, before going to bed about eleven o'clock.

FRI. 7. Went up to see Mrs Packman tonight or rather I should say, the Miss Packmans, their mother being with her husband, Captain Packman, at Alloa, from which place he sailed this morning at one o'clock for Genoa. She came home tonight when I was there, very tired with her journey, having gone down with her husband from Alloa to Leith, and in consequence did not get to bed all last night. Got to bed about eleven o'clock, that is me and not Mrs Packman.

SAT. 8. Got off at two o'clock as usual and started with the quarter past three train to go out to my father's where I arrived about five o'clock.

SUN. 9. Lay in bed till nine o'clock, then went to the church in the forenoon as usual and started at five o'clock for Dundee. Came in by the Kellas as usual and got a fine pleasant chat with Anne. Not being like to get one in the house and it being a rainy night and particularly heavy the time I was there, what did Anne do but get an umbrella, when we both went out and got a nice quiet crack together. So if that isn't 'umbrella courtship' as Anne said it was, I don't know what is. Got home a little before ten o'clock.

MON. 10. Wrote a letter to my cousin Andrew Petrie tonight and then intended to have a while at my journal, filling up, but getting started in conversation with my bed-fellow, I only got two or three lines done and did not get to bed till twelve o'clock either.

TUES. 11. Got a letter from John Wright today in which he was telling me that he was getting tired of Coupar Angus already and wishing he was back to Dundee again. Was away out the Perth Road seeing Mary Findlay tonight and did not get home till about half past ten, and then took a while at my journal, filling up, and got to bed about half past eleven.

WED. 12. Wrote a letter to my cousin in America and sat and chatted with my bed-fellow and did not get to bed till half past eleven.

THURS. 13. Wrought till quarter to seven tonight, then went along to the Post Office with the letter for my cousin. Went down and had a look at the shipping in the docks. Took a walk to and round the Camperdown Dock and got home about half past nine. Took a look at the newspapers and a while at my books, filling up, and got to bed about eleven o'clock.

FRI. 14. Went in the town and down to the Greenmarket where I purchased Walker and Webster's *Pronouncing Dictionary of the English Language*, which I saw last night and thought it was too good a bargain to let slip, the price of it being only four shillings. I then took a look round the docks and came up the town again where I met George Milne and had a while's conversation with him, when he told me that he had left the foundry tonight, his apprenticeship having expired tonight. Got home at nine o'clock and took a look at my dictionary before going to bed at eleven o'clock.

SAT. 15. Got off at two o'clock and went off at four on a pleasure excursion up the river with the steam tug *Atlas*. Touched at Newburgh to allow any that desired it to get off there then held up as far as Perth, but having no time to stop, it just turned round and came down again. Stopped a few minutes at Newburgh and arrived in Dundee exactly at ten o'clock. Very highly pleased with my afternoon's excursion there being nothing to mar our enjoyment except some showers shortly after we started, after which it cleared up pretty well so that we got a good view of the grand and imposing scenery with which both sides of our beautiful river is adorned. I could easily spend another Saturday afternoon the same way which I perhaps will yet before the summer is through. Did a little to my books, filling up, after I got home and then chatted a while with my bed-fellow and did not get to bed till past twelve o'clock.

SUN. 16. Got up at seven o'clock and as usual took a walk in the Baxter Park before breakfast. Went along to St John's, Mr Laird's church, in the forenoon where I saw Mary and David Findlay and came along to the High Street with them, where I met my bed-fellow and had a walk along the Marine Parade with him, and then went along together and heard Mr McGregor in the afternoon, where I saw and had a few minutes' conversation with Helen Wright. Took a look at the *Sunday Magazine* after tea and then went and heard Mr McGillvray of the Mains in Chapelshade, where I saw and stopped a short time with an old acquaintance of the name of William Kydd. Met John and Mrs McKinnes as I was coming home and went up with them to their house at the top of Dens Brae and stopped till about ten o'clock with them. Got to bed a little before eleven.

MON. 17. Got a letter from my cousin Thomas Petrie this morning. Took a while at my journal, filling up, after tea and spent the rest of the evening in doing sundry little nick-nacks not worth mentioning and did not go to bed till half past eleven.

TUES. 18. Wrote and went to the Post Office with a letter to Anne, then took a look at the newspapers before going to bed about eleven o'clock.

WED. 19. Went up to Mrs McHardy's where I stopped till about quarter to ten and got to bed about the half hour past it.

THURS. 20. Went in the town to the High Street, then down and round the docks and along to the Victoria and Camperdown Docks, which were opened today by the ship, *George Gilroy*, belonging to Gilroy Brothers, from Calcutta with jute. It presented a beautiful appearance on entering the docks, being all hung over with flags and bunting from stem

to stern, besides being manned by a detachment of the Royal
Naval Reserve, who greatly heightened its appearance by being
stationed in true naval fashion out at the extreme ends of the
yard arms. After taking a look at it and having a walk round the
Dock, I went out the Ferry Road a bit, then up and through the
Baxter Park along the front of the Morgan Hospital and looked
a few minutes at it and got home at half past nine, and after
lounging about a while and scrawling down this sketch of my
evening's walk I got to bed at eleven o'clock.

FRI. 21. Wrought till eight o'clock tonight and then took a
look at the bi-weekly *Advertiser* which I bought today for the
purpose of sending to my uncle in America to let him see the
particulars of the opening of the new docks yesterday. Did not
get to bed till half past eleven.

SAT. 22. Got off at two o'clock as usual and then went out to
my father's, taking the train to Monifieth as usual and arrived
at the Monument about five o'clock.

SUN. 23. Got up at eight o'clock and went out and enjoyed
the fresh morning air before breakfast in company with Charles
McHardy, a cousin of my father's and a native of Dundee, who
came out with his wife last night, who is to stop for a week
at my father's for the benefit of her health, as she has not
been very strong for some time past. We also had a visit from
my grandfather from Forfar today and also my uncle Charles
and his wife and my aunt Joan and her husband, William
McKenzie, so there was quite a full house at the Monument
today. They started on their way home again about half past
six, and Charles McHardy and I left for Dundee at a quarter to
seven. We came in by the Drumsturdy road and in consequence
I was disappointed of seeing and getting a crack with my dear
Anne and sorely disappointed her also no doubt, as she was
expecting me tonight. We got home about a quarter past nine
and not getting my midway rest as usual I was pretty tired.
Was at church in the forenoon as usual.

MON. 24. Loitered about looking out at the window for a
while after tea and then went in the town with my bed-fellow
and sauntered about a while. Was along at the station also and
saw a number of the Arbroath excursionists leaving, of whom
there has been a great number in town today. Got home again
a little past nine and sat and looked out at the window again

till ten and then commenced to my books, filling up, and did not get to bed till twelve o'clock.

TUES. 25. Went out to the Kellas tonight to see Anne, with whom I stopped till twelve o'clock and got home about a quarter past one.

WED. 26. Wrought tonight till a quarter past two putting a new drum in the turning shop.

THURS. 27. Went down the town with my watch of which the main spring was broken. Saw Margaret Wright and had a while's conversation with her and got home at half past eight and took a while at my books, filling up, before going to bed about ten o'clock.

FRI. 28. Went and called on Mr and Mrs Peter Kydd in the Hawkhill with whom I once lodged for a while. Got home about ten o'clock and was not long in going to bed.

SAT. 29. Got off at two o'clock as usual and started at a quarter past three with the steam tug *Atlas* on a trip to St Andrews. Had a very pleasant sail down the river; passed close to the wreck of the *Dalhousie* and arrived there about six o'clock. But as we had little more than an hour and a quarter to stop, there was no time for seeing anything hardly, but as far as I saw of it, I think it is well worth spending a day in, there being some grand old ruins in it, which are almost worth going to see themselves. We arrived in Dundee again at half past ten after a somewhat long voyage of three hours, the wind being directly against the steamer coming home and very bitter cold till we got up the river a good bit, when it was not quite so bad. Took a look at the newspapers after I came home and got to bed a little before twelve.

SUN. 30. Got up at seven o'clock and went east to the Stannergate and had a bath before breakfast. Went and heard Mr Knight of Free St Enoch's in the forenoon and started about one o'clock and went out to my sister's at Monifieth where I have not been for a good while past now. Found Mr Sturrock Arthur there and also Mrs Arthur, who has been stopping there for a few days past, and is to take another two or three yet. Mr Arthur and I started a little before seven to come home and arrived in Dundee about twenty minutes past eight. I went along to his house with him and had a crack with Mrs McHardy and him for a while and got down to my lodgings a little past nine. Had a while's conversation with my bed-fellow and a brother of his who stopped with us all night, and did not get to bed till past twelve o'clock.

MON. 31. Took a while at my books, filling up, and then wrote a letter to John Wright, and did not get to bed till past twelve o'clock.

AUGUST

TUES. 1. Wrote a letter to Anne tonight and got to bed about a quarter to eleven.

WED. 2. Went in the town on some errands tonight, then down to the docks and looked about me a while and was home again by nine o'clock. Then read a while at the *Sunday Magazine* for August which I bought tonight and got to bed about eleven o'clock.

THURS. 3. Went in the town for my watch tonight but did not get it. It is not to be ready till Saturday now. I then went down and along Dock Street, round Camperdown Dock and up and had a walk through the Baxter Park and was home about nine o'clock and read a while at Dick's *Christian Philosopher* before going to bed about eleven o'clock.

FRI. 4. Went up to Mrs McHardy's tonight and had a crack with John Gibson a while. Then came along to her daughter's, Mrs Arthur, where I stopped till ten o'clock. Then took a while at my books, filling up, and got to bed about eleven.

SAT. 5. Got off at two as usual and started with the quarter past three train for Monifieth on my way to my father's.

SUN. 6. Got up at eight o'clock and went out and had a walk before breakfast. Went to church as usual in the forenoon. Felt a little drowsy about the beginning of the sermon, but on the whole was not half so bad as I have been for some time past. In fact, I might say since ever the warm weather commenced. Went along to my brother David's at Panmure after dinner and spent the afternoon with them and started at quarter to seven for Dundee. Came in the old or Drumsturdy road and arrived home about nine o'clock, it having rained pretty heavy for the last three miles, which made me step out rather smarter than I would otherwise have done. Got to bed at half past ten.

MON. 7. Got a letter from John Wright tonight with which I

was particularly well pleased and which was also a particularly long one, having filled to a few lines two whole sheets of paper. Went up and called on Charles McHardy tonight where I spent a very happy and pleasant evening, both him and his wife being very kind and delighted-like with me. They also took and introduced me to Mr John Yeadon, who is inspector for the whole of Scotland for a steam engine and boiler insurance company. He is a very nice frank sort of fellow and one from whom a great deal of useful information could be got in the course of conversation. I got home at a quarter to eleven, had a little conversation with my bed-fellow, a while at my books, filling up, and got to bed at half past twelve.

TUES. 8. Wrought all night.

WED. 9. Got a letter from my dear Anne tonight in which she was expressing her regret at having to disappoint me in not going along with me to my father's on Sunday first, as she had promised. Her reason for it is that it was that day two years on which she lost her dear mother. All honour to you, my darling Anne, for your kind remembrance of your mother. Little incidents such as that tends to strengthen my love for you every day, Anne, and to long most earnestly for the time that shall make you mine. Yes, dear Anne, often, often, do I look forward to and long for that happy day. Went in the town tonight for my watch and took a walk up Reform Street and round the High Street and was home again by eight o'clock. Did a little to my journal, filling up, etc., etc., and went to bed at half past nine.

THURS. 10. Spent the most part of the evening in reading and then wrote a few lines of a letter to my father and brought forward my journal and got to bed about a quarter past eleven.

FRI. 11. Trifled away about an hour after tea without doing anything, then started to the tailoring business and sewed on two or three buttons and mended some cracks and flaws, etc., and had a while's discussion and conversation with my bed-fellow before going to bed about eleven o'clock.

SAT. 12. Got off at two o'clock as usual and went out to the Baxter Park after dinner where I stopped till six o'clock, when I came home and got tea and then went in the town for a while and had a stroll here and there for a short time and then went

east to and had a walk round the Camperdown Dock in which
there are three very large vessels lying at present, which are
well worth going to see. I then came west the south side of
the docks and up through the Greenmarket to High Street
where I stopped a short time and got home about a quarter
past nine. Took a while at the newspapers and filled up my
books for the night and got to bed about half past eleven.

SUN. 13. Got up at half past seven and had a walk in the Baxter
Park before breakfast. Went and heard Mr Knight of Free
St Enoch's in the forenoon and afternoon. Took a walk round
the docks and along the Marine Parade between the services and
heard Mr Riddle, Cameronian minister, in Free Chapelshade in
the evening who delivered a very earnest and impressive sermon
from the words: 'Who hath blessed us with all spiritual blessings
in heavenly places in Christ'. It was listened to by a very large
and attentive audience. I got home about a quarter past eight,
took a look at Brown's *Self-Interpreting Bible* and read some
pieces here and there and got to bed at half past ten.

MON. 14. Wrote a letter to my cousin Andrew Sturrock,
chatted a while to my bed-fellow occasionally, and took a
while at my journal, filling up, and did not get to bed till
almost twelve o'clock.

TUES. 16. Went to my manager's, John Sturrock, tonight
where I stopped till ten o'clock. Got to bed about eleven.

WED. 17. Went up to Mrs McHardy's tonight with some
butter for her which came in my box yesterday. Was home
again by half past eight and not having been very well today I
sat down and rested myself a while and then took a look over
some of the first of my journal and made some corrections in
it. Filled up a part of this and got to bed about ten o'clock.

THURS. 17. Went along to Constitution Road tonight to see
Margaret Wright. Her sister Helen came in while I was there
with whom I went along to the west end of the Magdalen Green
where she is stopping at present. Got home at half past ten and
got to bed about eleven.

FRI. 18. Was at a supper at the Albion Hotel tonight
with the manager, several of the foremen and a number
of the engine fitters and millwrights of Lilybank Foundry,
23 in all, on the occasion of three engines starting. We
spent a very pleasant evening together and broke up a

few minutes past eleven. Got home at twenty minutes to twelve.

SAT. 19. Got off at two o'clock as usual and then went out to my father's at Panmure Monument.

SUN. 20. Got up at eight o'clock and started at nine to go and meet my Anne, who was coming to go to church with me today. I went along the length of Denhead, although from the nature of the day which was very dull and somewhat rainy I did not expect her to come. However I stopped till a quarter past ten, after which I thought she would not come, but imagine my surprise at seeing her in the church when I went in. I could scarcely believe my eyes. She did not get away at the time she intended and not knowing the road up to the Monument, she just stopped at the church. She came up with us of course after the service and spent the afternoon at the Monument and started between six and seven to go home again, accompanied of course by myself. We arrived at the Kellas at eight after a pretty pleasant walk and a nice quiet crack by ourselves and something sweet to season it with of course. I stopped about half an hour or so at the Kellas and arrived in Dundee at ten o'clock. Got to bed at eleven.

MON. 21. Spent the evening at the newspapers and my books, filling up, etc. etc. Got to bed about eleven o'clock.

TUES. 22. Spent the evening at my manager's, Mr John Sturrock's, house who has very kindly offered to give me some instruction and lessons in connection with my trade, etc., etc.

WED. 23. Went in the town and got my hair cut. Took a walk round the docks and had a look at the shipping, etc. Got home at half past nine and read a while before going to bed about eleven.

THURS. 24. Spent the evening at Mr Sturrock's.

FRI. 25. Went in the town with my bed-fellow tonight and then went east Dock Street to have a look at the shows, etc., which are here on the occasion of the Fair and annual holidays. Went in to three or four of them, some of which were worth seeing and some were not. Happened to meet two of my bed-fellow's weavers (he is a tenter) with whom we chatted a while and then took a walk round by the High Street together on our way home, they stopping in King Street. Got home at half past ten, scrawled a few lines in my journal and got to bed about a quarter past eleven.

SAT. 26. Wrought till eleven o'clock tonight at James Irons' Mill where I commenced at two o'clock in the afternoon.

SUN. 27. Did not get up till a quarter to nine today. Went to Wellgate Territorial Church in the forenoon, St Enoch's in the afternoon and Chapelshade in the evening. Commenced a letter to my Anne in the afternoon and finished it in the evening. Got to bed about eleven as usual.

MON. 28. Wrought till ten o'clock at James Irons' Mill.

TUES. 29. Commenced at five o'clock at Mill today and wrought till ten again.

WED. 30. Wrought all night and got home about eight o'clock on the morning of the 31st, and after getting some breakfast and myself cleaned I went in the town between ten and eleven. Went down to the shore and had a nice warm bath which I enjoyed very much, and after looking about me for a while I got home at half past one and then read at the *Sunday Magazine*, which I bought today, till about three, when I went up to Mrs Packman's and stopped till about half past five and was not long home when John Wright came in. He got home from Coupar Angus on Saturday last and went off on Monday afternoon on an excursion to Glasgow from which he returned this afternoon and being on his way out to his father's I went out to Midmill with him and got home again a little before nine. Did a little to my books, filling up, and got to bed about half past ten.

SEPTEMBER

FRI. 1. Got up about seven o'clock and started at half past eight for the Kellas where I arrived at ten with the intention of stopping all forenoon and then starting after dinner for the Monument. But it turned out to be a pretty late dinner time indeed, for I did not get away till seven o'clock, a good part of the time of course being spent with my darling Anne.

SAT. 2. Got up about a quarter to seven and started a little before nine to go up to my brother William's at Carmyllie who by the by has been down at the Buddon with our brother James for the last nine or ten days and from what I have heard he has been rather better since he went down and a good deal readier for his food since he went down than what he used to be. But for all that I am like to think that his working days are done, poor fellow. My brother Alexander at Guilday was just commencing his harvest when I went over and I stopped all forenoon with him and gave him a little assistance. Had already had about an hour and a half or two hours shearing and have been feeling the effects of it all this day, Monday, yet got up to Carmyllie between two and three o'clock. I also went up in the evening and saw my uncle and aunt and got a crack with them.

SUN. 3. Got up about seven o'clock again and started a little before eight for the Monument in company with my brother Robert, William's wife having started at the same time for the Buddon to see her husband. Went and heard Mr McIntyre as usual. Started at five o'clock for the Kellas. Got a long quiet crack with my Anne and left at half past seven for Dundee where I arrived about nine. Had a while's conversation with my bed-fellow and did not get to bed till a quarter to eleven.

MON. 4. Spent the evening at the newspapers and my book, filling up. Got to bed about eleven o'clock as usual.

TUES. 5. Spent the evening at Mr J. Sturrock's.

WED. 6. Spent the evening at Mrs Packman's in company with J. Wright, then went along to the top of the Marraygate with him and got home at ten o'clock.

THURS. 7. Spent the evening at Mr J. Sturrock's. Got a call from my dear Anne today at dinner time, but which was of course a short one, it being nearly three oclock when she called and which was merely to let me know that she was expecting to be in town again on Sunday in company with her brother George and Miss Dykes.

FRI. 8. Went out to the Baxter Park tonight where there was a Grand Flower Show today in commemoration of the opening of the same. The show was open to the public this afternoon and is to be all tomorrow also. I went in and saw it tonight and was quite delighted with it. It was in my opinion a splendid collection both of flowers and vegetables, there being some specimens of the latter which I could call perfect monsters. There were also some beautiful bouquets and floral devices. Went up to Mrs Packman's a few minutes as I was coming home and got Elizabeth's and Margaret's cards. Got home

about twenty minutes to ten, filled up a bit of my journal
and got to bed about twenty past eleven.

SAT. 9. Got off at two o'clock as usual and went up with my
sisters Ann and Isabella (who come into town this morning)
to the Baxter Park. Went through the flower show with them
and round the park and then came down and got some tea
after which we went up to the Bucklemaker Wynd and called
on Charles McHardy and then went in the town to look about
for a while. Happened to meet first Helen and then Margaret
Wright with whom we strolled about here and there till ten
o'clock at which time we all separated on the High Street. I then
went up with my sisters to Mrs McHardy's, where they stopped
all night. Took a while at the newspapers after I came home
and did not get to bed till about quarter or twenty to twelve.

SUN. 10. Lay in bed till eight o'clock today and even then I was
very unwilling to get up, having got very little sleep all night from
my stomach having got over-loaded and out of order someway
or other, so much so that I have not taken above as much food
all day as would be one ordinary diet, the very sight of it being
quite enough for me. Went up at nine o'clock with my sisters to
Charles McHardy's to our breakfast to which we were invited
last night. Stopped till about half past ten when I went along
to Mrs Packman's where I was expecting to see my Anne with
her brother George and Miss Dykes, but they did not arrive till
eleven o'clock and then they all went away to church, except
Mrs Packman and George, with whom I stopped a while and
then came along to Sturrock Arthur's where my sisters were
and went along with them to the west end of the town to
call on a cousin, Jane McKenzie, Mrs Stratton. Landed at
Mrs Packman's again a little past two, with my sisters, after
which we all set out together and had a walk in the Baxter
Park where we stopped till tea time, my sisters and I going to
Sturrock Arthur's to ours. We went along for a while again to
Mrs Packman's from where they all started a little before six
for home. I went out the length of Midmill with my sisters,
but the Kellas folk having their gig with them had been nearly
home by the time we got there. I got home between seven and
eight and went to bed about a quarter to nine, as I was both
tired and sleepy, not having been anything like well all day.
Did not get a quiet crack with my Anne today at all.

MON. 11. Wrought till ten o'clock tonight and then did a little to my journal, filling up, before going to bed. Met my cousin Thomas Petrie as I was going up to my work at dinner time. He came in to the town in the forenoon and had been looking about for a while for my lodgings but without success. He went up to the foundry with me, when I got permission to show him through it, and he not having seen anything of the kind before was quite delighted with it. Better today than what I was yesterday but not quite right yet.

TUES. 12. Working till ten o'clock again then took a while at my journal and did not get to bed till twelve o'clock. Got about all right again this afternoon.

WED. 13. Working till ten o'clock again and then wrote a few lines of a letter to J. Wright and got to bed about half past eleven.

THURS. 14. Ten o'clock again.

FRI. 15. Do.

SAT. 16. Got off at two o'clock as usual and then went down with the quarter past three train to Monifieth, then went along to my sister's, Clementina's, at the South Grange, where I stopped a while and got up to the Monument between seven and eight. Got a rise of three shillings on my wages today, which now makes them 19*s*. per week. I was expecting to get a rise for some weeks past but never expected to get more than two at the outside and was quite surprised and need hardly say delighted too when I saw three shillings instead of two more than usual.

SUN. 17. Lay in bed till nine o'clock today. Went and heard Mr McIntyre as usual and was particularly pleased with him today. Started at five o'clock for the Kellas, where of course I had to stop a while and exchange a few sweet words with my darling Anne. Got company in with Margaret Packman and Ann Findlay. Went down to the Shore Terrace with the latter and was up to my lodgings again by half past nine and was in bed by a quarter to eleven. Got an invitation today to my brother Robert's wedding and at which I have to act as best man.

MON. 18. Went in the town tonight and bought a new necktie for the marriage, also a bottle of port wine which I intend to give him in a present. Was home again a quarter past eight and took a while at my books, filling up, and did not get to bed till almost half past eleven.

TUES. 19. Went along and called on J. Wright with whom I spent the evening till almost ten o'clock. He then came along the length of the Murraygate with me when we went into Mathers' Temperance Hotel and had a pie and ginger beer. Got home at half past ten, took a while at the newspapers and got to bed about the same time as last night.

WED. 20. Went up to Mr Allan's in Church Street, the father of my brother's intended wife, to make some arrangements about the marriage on Friday. Stopped till about a quarter to ten, filled up a bit of my journal and got to bed about a quarter to eleven.

THURS. 21. Spent the evening at Mr John Sturrock's, came home about a quarter past nine and trifled about and did not get to bed till about half past eleven.

FRI. 22. This being my brother's marriage day I did not go to work at all, but took an extra hour in bed, namely till half past six, and then went in the town and looked about a while and took a walk round the docks, both old and new, and got home again about half past eight. Got breakfast and dressed myself and went down to the station and met Robert who arrived at five minutes to ten, accompanied by George and Isabella. Robert and I then went to the Register Office, engaged two cabs to take us to the station and got up to Church Street at half past ten. Got through with the ceremony at half past eleven, got some dinner and got down to the station in time for the ten minutes to one train for Carnoustie, and then walked up to his house at the Milton of Carmyllie, where we arrived about half past three, and kept up the sport to between two and three o'clock in the morning, after which I went home with a lass of the name of Margaret Ramsay to the Goat, a small farm belonging to her father and about a mile or so from the Milton. We sat down and had a while's chatting together before I came away again and I did not get back to the Milton till almost five o'clock when I got to bed as quickly as possible and lay till nine on Saturday morning and after getting breakfast I went up to Greystone to see my brother William, who is strictly speaking not likely to get much better yet. I had only time to stop about an hour or so at Greystone as I had to see a young girl, Christina Chambers, a niece of my brother's wife, down to the station at Carnoustie by a quarter to three o'clock, and as I have to be out at the Monument on Saturday first, I just came up along with her and did not go to my father's at all. Came up with Miss Chambers to her grand-father's, Mr Allan's, and stopped about half an hour or so and then went in the town to meet my brother George who came up with us. Met him at the top of the Murraygate and brought him up to my lodgings to get some tea. Went in the town again and looked about us till half past six at which time he left with the train on his way home. Was accosted as I was making my way home by a son of William Lumgairs, Kerrystone Bank, who asked me if I knew anything about some lodgings which he had been hearing about and which he was in want of and as I happened to be acquainted with the landlady, an aunt of John Wright's, Mrs Weir, I went up with him to her house, the same being exactly on my road coming home and where of course I had to stop a while. Got home about a quarter to eight, took a while at my books, filling up, a while at the newspaper and got to bed about a quarter to eleven, being both pretty tired and sleepy by that time.

SUN. 24. Lay in bed till eight o'clock today and did not go out to take a walk before breakfast as I usually do but spent the time at the *Sunday Magazine* reading. Went and heard Mr Knight of Free St Enoch's in the forenoon and afternoon. Took a walk along the Marine Parade and out the Nethergate to the Magdalen Green between the services. Wrote a few lines of a letter to my darling Anne after tea, then went along to Free Chapelshade and heard an excellent sermon from Mr William of St Paul's on the parable of the servant who received a talent from his master and then went out and hid it in the earth, and thus abused it instead of using it. Met John Wright as I was coming home and turned and went along to the old Newtyle Station with him and got home at nine o'clock. Read a while at the *Sunday Magazine*, etc., and got to bed about a quarter to eleven.

MON. 25. Went up to Mr Allan's tonight for some parcels to send out with the carrier tomorrow. Got home at a quarter to nine, took a while at my journal and got to bed at a quarter to eleven.

TUES. 26. Went up to Mr Sturrock's tonight where I stopped till about half past nine, then took a while at my journal and got to bed at eleven.

WED. 27. Went out to the Kellas tonight to see and get a crack with my dear Anne. Also went in and stopped a while with her brother James and got home about a quarter past twelve.

THURS. 28. Went in the town tonight and bought for myself a small spirit level and pair of trammel heads for James Sturrock. Happened to meet J. Wright with whom I went into the Restaurant and had a bottle of ginger beer and a game or two at draughts. Got home at a quarter past ten and to bed at eleven.

FRI. 29. Spent the evening at home practising a little at the drawing. Got to bed about eleven.

SAT. 30. Got off at two o'clock as usual and then went out to my father's. Started with the quarter past three train.

OCTOBER

SUN. 1. Lay in bed till nine o'clock today and then went and heard Mr McIntyre as usual. My brother Robert and his wife being giving them a call at the Monument today and also my cousins Thomas and John Petrie from Mill of Lour, I did not get started for Dundee till a quarter past six and being too late then for having any time to stop at the Kellas I took the Newsbigging and Drumsturdy road on which I have no calls to make and got home at a quarter to nine o'clock and took a look at the *Sunday Magazine* before going to bed about half past ten.

MON. 2. Went in the town and bought some little trifles and then up to Lamb's Lane, Bucklemaker's Wynd, and called on Charles McHardy. Got home a little past ten, took a while at my books, filling up, and got to bed about a quarter past eleven.

TUES. 3. Spent the evening at Mr Sturrock's till twenty minutes to ten. Got to bed at eleven.

WED. 4. Went in the town and put three pounds in the bank, and then went along to call on J. Wright, who happened to be away at Arbroath where he is to be for two or three days. Came direct home again where I arrived at eight o'clock and then took a look at the *Sunday Magazine*, which I bought as I was coming up. Got to bed at half past eleven.

THURS. 5. Spent the evening at home practising a little of my arithmetic (decimals). Got to bed about half past ten.

FRI. 6. Spent the evening at Mr Sturrock's till half past nine, then took a look at Molesworth's *Formulae* and got to bed about a quarter past eleven. Got a few lines of a letter from my dear Anne tonight in which she was telling me that she and her father and her brother's wife and children had been all up at Carmyllie together and that she saw not all of *my* friends but all of *our* friends. Yes dear Anne they are ours, for though we are not yet united in the bonds of marriage, I even now look on myself as being as much yours at the present time as if we were so, and that little word 'ours', a thousand thanks to you for it, Anne, for I have no words to express the happiness and joy or pleasure which it gave me, for it conveyed to me the joyful assurance so plainly and frankly, much more I think than ever you gave me before, that you are mine. Yes, dear Anne, and that you look upon yourself as being so even now and which I fervently hope we will continue to do as long as God sees fit to spare us for each other. It is now within a few minutes of twelve.

SAT. 7. Got off at two o'clock as usual and then went in the town after dinner and saw the Rifle Volunteers assemble in front of the High Schools at four o'clock, after which I looked about me a while and went down and took a walk round the docks, both old and new, and got home to tea at a quarter to six. Went in the town again in the evening to a Grand Concert of first class artistes in the Corn Exchange Hall who were engaged for the inauguration of the new organ which has been put up there. Got home at twenty minutes to eleven, filled up a little at my books and got to bed about a quarter to twelve.

SUN. 8. Lay in bed till eight o'clock this morning and then went out and took a walk through the Baxter Park before breakfast. Went and heard Mr Knight of Free St Enoch's both forenoon and afternoon, with whom I was particularly well pleased today. Came home in the middle of the day and took a look at the *Sunday Magazine*. Went with my bed-fellow to Sturrock Arthur's after tea, where we stopped a short time and then went down and heard Mr Spence of Ward Road Independent Chapel. Went up and met John Wright at the end of Victoria Street and went in the town a bit with him and got home again at nine o'clock and after reading a while at the *Sunday Magazine* and a chapter and psalm, which I always do on Sunday night. I got to bed at half past ten.

MON. 9. Went down to the High Street tonight to meet J. Wright with whom I made an engagement last night. But owing I suppose to its being a heavy night of rain he did not come. At least I did not see him, so I got home again by eight o'clock and after filling up a bit of my journal and writing a letter to my darling Anne I got to bed at half past eleven.

TUES. 10. Spent the evening at Mr Sturrock's till twenty minutes to ten. Took a look at Molesworth's *Formulae*, had a while's conversation with my bedfellow and got to bed at eleven.

WED. 11. Went and heard the first of course of lectures to be given under the auspices of the Young Men's Christian Association which was delivered by the Rev. William Arnot, Edinburgh, subject: 'The Dundee Young Men's Christian Association', which he handled in a very eloquent and masterly manner. Got home at ten o'clock, filled up a little of my books and got to bed about eleven.

THURS. 12. Wrought till a quarter past seven tonight then took a while at the drawing and got to bed a little before eleven.

FRI. 13. Spent the evening at drawing again. Was making a sketch of a vertical boring machine, which I have got finished tonight. Got to bed about eleven.

SAT. 14. Got off at two o'clock as usual and tomorrow being the Sacrament I went down to church after dinner and got my token. Got out at half past four and after buying a cravat and looking about a while I got home to tea about half past five, after which I went down to the High Street again and then along to the Arbroath Station with my brother George who was in town today. Came back to the High Street again by way of Greenmarket and took a stroll along the Nethergate, Reform Street, etc., and was home again by a quarter to eight. I forgot to mention last night that I saw and got a short conversation with my Anne yesterday at dinner time who was in town along with her father who I suppose was not aware that it was principally to see me that Anne came along with him yesterday. I said in the letter which I wrote to her in the beginning of the week that perhaps I would be out on Friday to see and get a crack with her. So she, so kind-living and mindfull of me, could not think of letting me come so far, as she always says, to see her and so soon after getting a letter too, so she took the opportunity to come in with her father, under shelter of some little errands of course, and so keep me from coming out. Many thanks to you, dear Anne, for your tender regard for my comfort. Spent the rest of the evening after coming home at the newspapers and my books, filling up, and did not get to bed till half past eleven.

SUN. 15. Got up at half past seven and had a walk through the Baxter Park as usual before breakfast. Joined myself today to Mr Knight's Free St Enoch's congregation, with whom I partook of the Sacrament. He was assisted by one, Professor Douglas of Glasgow, who served both the tables but of whose addresses I could make little or nothing. Mr Knight then gave a very instructive and solemn closing address which was so plain and clear that anyone I think could have understood it. The service concluded a little before three o'clock and commenced again a quarter past six. Spent much of the intervening time reading the *Sunday Magazine*. Professor Douglas conducted the service and gave an excellent discourse with which I was highly pleased. Met a shop-mate, Alex Robertson, as I was coming home and had a while's conversation with him, when John Wright came up, with whom I went in the town a bit and got home at half past nine and got to bed about an hour after.

MON. 16. Spent the evening at home taking a turn-over among my clothes, packing up my dirty ones and doing some little jobs at the tailoring business, but which would have been far better done by a dear girl whom I hope to have one day yet to do them for me. Took a while at my books, filling up, and got to bed about eleven o'clock.

TUES. 17. Went and heard the second of the course of lectures tonight which was delivered by James Dodds, Esq., London, subject: 'How England and Scotland met the Spanish Armada in 1588'. It was on the whole a splendid lecture but not nearly so interesting to me as what the first one was. Got home at ten o'clock and got to bed at eleven.

WED. 18. Spent the evening at Mr Sturrock's where I stopped till ten o'clock. Then did a little to my books, filling up, then got to bed about eleven.

THURS. 19. Wrought to half past eight tonight, then mended one of my braces, and took a look at today's *Advertiser* and got to bed about eleven o'clock.

FRI. 20. Spent the most of the evening reading the *English Mechanic*, a journal which I have commenced to take, and which is a weekly record of mechanical inventions and scientific and industrial progress. Had a while's conversation also with a Mr Caird, a friend of my bed-fellow's, who was calling on him tonight in company with his young wife, he having got married on Monday last, previous to his leaving for a three years' engagement as mechanic on a power-loom factory in Spain. Did a little to my books, filling up also, and got to bed about a quarter past eleven.

SAT. 21. Got off at two o'clock as usual and left with the quarter past three train for Monifieth on my way to my father's where I arrived about five o'clock and found them all well.

SUN. 22. Lay in bed again till almost nine o'clock. Went to church as usual and heard one Mr Walker from Dundee, who gave an excellent sermon from the words, 'Having a desire to depart and to be with Christ which is far better'. Started about five o'clock as usual for the Kellas where I arrived a little past six and found Elizabeth Packman waiting for me. Stopped about an hour and half or so and of course contrived to get a few words with my dear Anne before leaving. Came in by Duntrune and also got company with John Wright and his sister Helen and arrived home at twenty minutes past nine and got to bed at half past ten.

MON. 23. Was up at Mr Sturrock's tonight, where I stopped till half past nine, then filled up a bit of my journal, read a while at the *English Mechanic* and got to bed at twenty minutes past eleven.

TUES. 24. Lecture night again. The lecturer tonight was the Rev. George Gilfillan, subject: 'The Moral and Religious Influence of Sir Walter Scott's Writings', and, more especially I think from what he said, of his novels, the *Waverley*, and from what he, the lecturer, said of their influence, if it is not great, at least ought to be so at any rate, and to give some idea of the estimation in which he himself holds them, he stated at the commencement of his lecture that there was not a day that passed but what he read a part of them and not a year but that he read them all from beginning to end. The lecture was on the whole a pretty interesting one. I got home a few minutes before ten took a while at the *English Mechanic* and got to bed at half past eleven.

WED. 25. Went and heard the great Italian patriot, the Rev. Alessandro Gavazzi, who delivered a lecture tonight in the Corn Exchange on 'Italy – Past, Present and Future' and which was one of the most powerful pieces of eloquence that ever I had the pleasure to hear. He intimated at the close of his lecture that he was to preach three different times in Dundee on Sabbath first and I intend at present to hear him all the three times again if possible. Got home at a quarter to ten, took a while at my journal, filling up, and got to bed about half past eleven.

THURS. 26. Went up with my bed-fellow to Victoria Street and called on a young lady, Miss Catherine Mill, from whom I had the loan of Dick's *Christian Philosopher*, to return which was my errand tonight. Got home about a quarter or twenty past ten, took a look at Milton's *Poems* and got to bed about half past eleven.

FRI. 27. Spent the evening at home reading the *English Mechanic*, etc. Got to bed about a quarter or twenty to eleven.

SAT. 28. Got off at two as usual. Then took a while at the newspapers after dinner and went in the town and looked about a while and had a walk round the docks and got home to tea about six o'clock. Went down again about half past seven and looked about a while and happened to meet Margaret and Helen Wright and another servant girl and some lads with them, where I halted a while and then came home with Margaret and the other girl, both of whom stopped in the Constitution Road. Got home at half past ten, filled up my books and got to bed at half past eleven.

SUN. 29. Got up about eight o'clock, but being a very heavy rain which continued till about mid-afternoon, I did not go out for a walk before breakfast, but employed the time in reading the *Sunday Magazine* for November which I bought last night. Went and heard the great Italian patriot and preacher, the Rev.

Alessandro Gavazzi, today. He preached in the forenoon in Mr Borwick's U.P. Church from the text, Romans 3 and 28: 'Therefore we conclude that a man is justified by faith without the deeds of the law'; in the afternoon in Mr Ewan's Free Church from I John 4 and 14: 'And we have seen and do certify that the Father sent the Son to be the Saviour of the world'; and in the evening in the Corn Exchange Hall from James 2 and 26: 'For as the body without the spirit is dead so faith without works is dead also'. They were three of the plainest and most practical sermons I think that ever I heard. He lays down his heads so plainly and clearly and illustrates them in so many different ways that anyone could understand them. Went up the length of Stobswell after the evening sermon expecting to meet John Wright, but did not see him. Got home at a quarter past eight, read a while at the *Sunday Magazine* and filled up my journal and got to bed about half past ten.

MON. 30. Went up to Mr Sturrock's where I stopped till half past eight, then went along to Mrs Packman's, where I stopped till about ten, after which I wrote a letter to my dear Anne, and did not get to bed till twelve o'clock.

TUES. 31. Went and heard Professor Nicoll from Glasgow deliver the fourth of the course of lectures tonight. The subject was 'Tennyson, Poet Laureate' and notwithstanding that he handled it in a very masterly manner it was not on the whole so interesting to me as what the others have been. Got home a little past ten, filled up my books, and got to bed about twenty past eleven.

NOVEMBER

WED. 1. Spent the evening at home reading the *English Mechanic*. Got to bed about half past eleven.

THURS. 2. Went along to J. Wright's lodgings in the Scouring-burn but did not see him, he not having got home today as he was expecting from Bullionfield Paper Works, where he has been all this week and also the last. I then came along to Constitution Road and called on his sister Margaret where I stopped till ten o'clock. Filled up a bit of my journal after coming home and got to bed about half past eleven.

FRI. 3. Took an evening's practice at arithmetic. Got to bed about half eleven as usual.

SAT. 4. Wrought tonight till eleven o'clock at Halley and Sons Mill, lighting cogs of flywheel.

SUN. 5. Got up at half past six, dressed myself and set out for the Kellas where I arrived at half past eight and got breakfast with James Sturrock after which I went down to see Anne and her father, and with whom I went to church and heard Mr Boyd. Got dinner with James again and went in the course of the afternoon and spent a time with my Anne, when I was telling her that I was quite tired and wearied of this cold and comfortless way of living in lodgings and that I should like a wife and home of my own now. She for her own part said she was quite ready and anxious to come and share it with me, except, kind tender-hearted creature that she is, she cannot see how she can leave her father, and indeed seeing how they're situated to each other I cannot blame her for it, but rather love her the more for her consideration for her father's comfort and happiness. So there is no other recourse but have patience and put up with lodgings a little longer yet. Got my tea with her father and her and then had an hour and a half or two hours conversation with them, and started a little past eight for Dundee again where I arrived at half past nine, having got company with John Wright from Midmill Bleachfield, where we happened to meet exactly together. Got to bed about half past ten.

MON. 6. Spent the evening at Mr Sturrock's till half past nine. Then filled up a bit of my journal and trifled about and did not get to bed till half past eleven.

TUES. 7. Went and heard Mr Ballantyne from Edinburgh deliver the fifth of the course of lectures. The subject was: 'Life among the Red Indians and Fur Traders of North America' and he having spent six years among them himself as governor of one of the Hudson Bay Company's forts he could speak from personal experience and gave some very interesting details of how they spent their time away out in these wild regions of the Far North and West. Got home about ten o'clock and sat down to read a while at the *English Mechanic*, but soon fell asleep and slept till almost half past eleven.

WED. 8. Had a visit from John Wright tonight with whom of

course I spent the evening in conversation and one thing or another till about half past ten, then went in the town a bit and got to bed about half past eleven as usual.

THURS. 9. Spent the evening at arithmetical practice . . . extraction of the square root. Took a while at my books, filling up, before going to bed about a quarter past eleven.

FRI. 10. Went in the town tonight and happened to meet John Wright and his father and his sister Helen with whom I came up to the top of King Street, John and his father being on their way out to Duntrune. I then went along with Helen to the west end of the Magdalen Green and got home again at half past nine. Read a little for amusement and made up my books for the night and got to bed a little past eleven.

SAT. 11. Got off at two o'clock as usual and started for the Kellas about half past three and arrived there at five, and being about Hallowe'en it was the intention to have a little sport there tonight. But as James Sturrock has been lying all the week, an attack of bronchitic gastritis and inflammation, we did not have so much sport as perhaps we might have had had he been well. However I got my tea with Anne, her father, her brother George and Miss Dykes, and then we four had a little sport together in the course of the evening. Miss Dykes left about ten o'clock and then Anne and I had a crack together, after which I went up to James's to bed about eleven o'clock.

SUN. 12. Got up about a quarter past seven and started for the Monument to my breakfast where I arrived about nine. James Sturrock had a very restless night and on the whole was rather worse than better. Went to the church as usual and being the Sacrament Day the service did not conclude till a quarter to four. Started for the Kellas at my usual time and I am sorry to say found James even worse than he was in the morning, so much so that I don't think he was sensible of my being in the room at all tonight. Got a word or two with my dear Anne before leaving, aye and a sweet kiss and a fond embrace too. Came in by Duntrune for J. Wright and arrived in Dundee about half past nine. Got to bed about half past ten.

MON. 13. Went along to Margaret Wright's tonight, and was one of a party of about a dozen which she had got permission to have on the occasion of Hallowe'en. Some of them who were keen for a dance went out and got hold of a blind fiddler, and his fiddle also of course, and we started dancing with such spirit that we kept up the sport till twelve o'clock. Filled up my income and expenditure book after I came home and got to bed at one o'clock.

TUES. 14. Lecture night again. The lecturer tonight was the Rev. J. P. Chawn of Bradford, subject: 'A Summer Furlough across the Atlantic', and which was in my opinion the best lecture of the whole series so far. It was in fact just a miniature trip to America and back again in less than two hours and at the same time one of the best descriptions of American manners, habits and customs that one could get, I think, without actually seeing it themselves. Got home at a quarter past ten, chatted a while with my bed-fellow and then filled up a bit of my journal and did not get to bed till twelve o'clock.

WED. 15. Spent the evening at Mr Sturrock's till ten o'clock. Then took a while at my journal again and got to bed at half past eleven.

THURS. 16. Was at soiree of employees of Lilybank Foundry tonight in Thistle Hall to which their employers, Messrs Pearce Brothers, were invited in compliment to them for their readiness and willingness in granting us the payment of our wages weekly instead of fortnightly. There were several excellent and appropriate speeches delivered, especially one by George Robb, draughtsman at the work, and the other by Mr James Reid, time-keeper. There were also several songs sung and on the whole the evening was spent in the most agreeable and harmonious manner imaginable and broke up, after enjoying an hour and a half's dancing, at twelve o'clock. Got home at twenty minutes past and was not long in getting to bed.

FRI. 17. Spent the entire evening at the fireside without doing anything except going down the street a few shops for a dose of castor oil which I am thinking of taking tomorrow as I have been very dry and bound up inside for some time and tonight I felt particularly tired and lazy like somehow and could not be troubled to do anything. So stopped the most of the evening at the fireside and after filling up a bit of my journal got to bed at eleven o'clock.

SAT. 18. Did not get off till about half past two today and after taking a look at the newspapers a while, I dressed myself and set off with the half past four train to my sister's at Monifieth, where I stopped till nine o'clock. Travelled up to Broughty Ferry and took the ten minutes to ten train and arrived at my lodgings here at half past. Took a look at the newspapers and got to bed at half past eleven.

SUN. 19. Lay in bed till half past eight and then spent the morning till church time reading the *Sunday Magazine*. Went to Free St Enoch's in the forenoon and afternoon and heard Mr McGregor of St Peter's in the Free Gaelic Church in the evening. The day being very wet and dirty I spent the whole time between the services at home principally reading the *Sunday Magazine*. Wrote a letter to my dear Anne after coming home in the evening and got to bed at eleven o'clock.

II

INCOME AND
EXPENDITURE
ACCOUNT, 1865

		£	S	D*
Jan 3	Money in hand	1	9	11½
7	Received from my brother William			
	to buy a hat for him		3	
9	Amount of Wages	2	0	11
21	" "	2	15	6
28	Price of hat from my father		2	6
Feb 4	Amount of Wages	1	15	8
18	" "	2	3	9
Mar 4	" "	1	19	1
18	" "	1	16	3
	Interest of ten pounds transferred from			
	Post Office to National Securities Savings			
	Banks		7	11
Apr 1	Amount of Wages	1	12	6
15	" "	1	16	2
29	" "	1	17	4
May 13	" "	1	16	5
27	" "	2	2	3
	Price of pot which I bought for my sister		3	8
Jun 10	Amount of Wages	1	5	1
23	" "	2	4	8
Jul 8	" "	1	12	4
22	" "	1	12	1
Aug 5	" "	1	15	11
19	" "	1	16	2
Sep 16	" "	2	19	5
30	" "	1	12	2
Oct 14	" "	1	19	2
28	" "	1	16	9
Nov 4	" "		14	8
11	" "	1	2	
18	" "		17	10
Dec 2	" "	1	15	8
18	" "	1	15	8
30	" "	1	17	4
Total amount of wages in 1865		52	4	3½

* Sums are given here in their contemporary form, i.e., in £ s. d. £1 = 100p. Therefore the first item, £1 9s 11½d = £1.50p in modern currency.

Jan 3	Newspaper and ginger beer		3
4	Sweetmeats and confectionery	1	1
	Sunday Magazine		7
	Wool lined gloves for present to my father	4	6
	Railway fare to Monifieth		6
5	Strong ale and sweeties	1	5
6	Strong ale and half glass of brandy		7
	Boots soling and repairing	4	
	Some coppers to James Sturrock's children, Kellas		2½
7	To my brother William's children, Carmyllie		2
	For two overall jackets and pair of trousers making	5	6
	To my mother for flannel shirt, butter, etc.		5
8	Church door collection		1
10	Board and lodging	12	9½
	Oranges and sweeties	1	
	Small portrait for locket and two cards	3	4
	Small account book and pass book		3
13	Cream of Tartar		1½
15	Strong ale and biscuit		4
	To subscription box for Wallace Monument fund in Castle Hill Cemetery, Stirling.		3
18	Five days board and lodging at Dunblane	6	6
	To keeper of Dunblane Cathedral		6
	Travelling expenses to and from Dunblane	9	2
	Porter and ginger beer		5
20	Oranges		3
21	Newspapers and church collection		1½
23	Board and lodging	10	3½
	Sweeties		3
24	For two hats for my father and brother William	6	
	For inside callipers or scribers		8
	Box of pills		2
	Lifeboat subscription		1
28	*People's Journal*		2
	Sweeties		3
29	Church door collection		½
28	Oxalic Acid		1
		3 16	11

Feb 1	Portraits of Horace Greely, Editor			
	of *New York Tribune*		1	
	Sunday Magazine			7
	Boots repairing			9
3	Black Sugar			2½
4	*People's Journal*			1
	Four linen collars		1	8
	Postage stamps			6
	Quarter pound of figs			2
	Bottle of ink			1
5	Church door collections			2
	Board and lodgings		13	6
7	Subscription for *People's Journal*			
	Lifeboat at foundry			2
11	*People's Journal*			1
	Bottle of marking ink			6
	Valentine			8
	Crabbe's *Poems*		3	6
	Scottish Reformation Society's annual			
	Festival ticket		1	
12	Church door collections			2
17	Bi-weekly *Advertiser*			2
18	*People's Journal*			1
	Sweeties			3
	Railway fare to Monifieth			6
20	Board and lodgings		14	2
25	*People's Journal*			1
	Apples			1
	Boots repairing		1	2
	Looking glass		1	2
	Sunday Magazine			7
26	Church collection			1½
		2	3	3

Mar	4	*People's Journal*		I
		Postage stamps		6
		Warm Bath		9
	5	Church door collections		2
	6	Board and lodging	13	4
		Sweeties		3
	7	Writing paper and envelopes		7
		Steel square	I	
	9	Biscuit		I
	10	Dinner at Coffee House		3
		Dress hat altering	3	6
	11	*People's Journal*		I
		Railway fare to Monifieth and sweeties		9
		Canvass for overalls	2	3
		For two draws or tickets for my brother William's lottery	2	
	12	Church door collection		I
	13	Dinner at Coffee House		2
	18	*People's Journal*		I
		Postage stamps		6
		Milton's *Poems*	2	6
		Mason on *Self Knowledge*	I	
		Sweeties		3
	19	Church door collection		7
	20	Board and lodging	12	4
		Hair cutting		2
	22	To cab driver for giving me a drive part of the road coming home from the Kellas (all I had on me)		2½
	23	To see Professor Pepper's Ghost		6
	24	For dinners at Coffee House – four days		8
	25	*People's Journal*		I
		Flannel for two shirts	6	3
		New stick for umbrella	I	9
		Oxalic acid		6
	26	Church door collection		I
		James Sturrock's little girl, Maggie		3
	30	Four days dinners at Coffee House		8
		Sunday Magazine		7
			2 14	9½

Apr 1	*People's Journal*		I
	Sweeties and biscuits		4
	Railway fare to Monifieth		6
	To my mother for butter and carriage of clothes out and in	3	8
2	Church door collection		I
3	Board and Lodging	12	3
7	Bi-weekly *Advertiser*		2
	Sweeties		3
8	*People's Journal*		I
	Pies, ginger beer and coffee for my brother George and myself	I	
	Quill pens		I
	Neck tie	2	
9	Church door collection		I
10	Sweeties		3
13	Daily *Advertiser*		I
15	*People's Journal*		I
	Dinner and coffee at Coffee House during the week	I	6
16	Church door collection		I½
17	Board and lodging	11	4
18	Postage stamps		6
	Bi-weekly *Advertiser*		2
19	Lotion for washing my eyes with		7
20	Pair of trammel heads	2	5
	2 pieces of steel for square blades	2	
	Joiner's pencil		I
	Pair of leather laces		I
22	*People's Journal*		I
	Sweeties		8
	Strong ale		9
	Railway fare to Monifieth		6
23	Church door collection		I
27	Daily *Advertiser*		I
29	*People's Journal*		I
	To poor man on the street		I
	Pair of Sunday boots	18	
30	Church door collection		2
		3 0	3½

May 1	Board and lodging		13	3
2	Daily *Advertiser*			1
6	*People's Journal*			1
	Board and lodging		5	8½
	To carter for removing my chest			7½
	New bonnet and necktie		2	
	Sweeties			3
	Admittance to Diorama in Corn Exchange Hall			6
7	Church door collections			2
13	Board and lodging		7	3½
	Railway to Monifieth			6
	Sweeties			3
	To my mother for butter, etc.		1	
	People's Journal			1
14	Church door collection			1
	To my sister Ann's boy			1
15	Pies and ginger beer			10
16	For a pot for my sister Clementina		3	8
	Piece of steel for square blade		1	6
	Plane iron			7
17	Black sugar			2
20	Board and lodging		6	4
	Postage stamps			6
	People's Journal			1
	To collection to defray expenses of Volunteer Band in Baxter Park			1
23	Admittance to Diorama front seat and two chances of prizes		1	
	Paper and envelopes as hansel to writing desk which Helen Wright gained at Diorama			8
26	Cough lozenges and figs			3
27	*People's Journal*			1
	Board and lodging		6	8
	For twelve cartes de visite of my sisters Ann and Mary		8	
	To black plaid which Ann, George and myself gave to my mother		10	
	To help my sister Mary to get boots		3	
	To Scots Bible binding and lost number containing Psalms and Paraphrases	1		

	Sweeties		10
	Ginger beer and biscuits		8
	Railway ticket to Monifieth		6
30	Sugar Candy		2½
31	Bottle of cough mixture		11
	Bottle of ginger beer		2
29	Bottle of castor oil and powder		8
		4	19 4

Jun 1	*Sunday Magazine*		7
	To poor man on street		½
3	*People's Journal*		1
	Board and lodging	6	6
3	Small portrait of Anne to put in locket	1	6
	Admittance for myself and Anne to Watt Museum		2
	Two cups of coffee with bread and bottle of ginger beer	1	2
	Sweeties		3½
	Two bottles of porter	1	
4	Church door collection		1
	To James Sturrock's girl at Kellas		1
5	Bottle of cough mixture	1	
	Cough lozenges		3
	Warm bath		6
	Dulse		½
7	Mustard for two blisters		4
10	*People's Journal* and railway time table		2
	Gloves dyeing		6
	Two bottles of lemonade		4
	Sweeties		3
	Railway fare to Monifieth		6
	Board and lodging	4	11½
11	Church door collection		1
13	Note book and book for my journal keeping, steel pens and pencil	1	2½
16	Six of my cartes de visite and one of Anne's	3	6
	Brooch repairing for my sister Mary		4
17	*People's Journal*		1
	Board and lodging	6	
	Joiner's pencil		1
	Dulse		½
	Pie and ginger beer		10
18	Church door collection		1
20	Bi-weekly *Advertiser*		2
23	Half mutchkin of port wine	1	4
	Sweeties		3
	Pair of leather laces		1
24	*People's Journal*		1
	Two railway return tickets to Perth	3	

	Pies, porter and wine in Perth	1		
	Walking stick bought in Perth		8	
	Two railway tickets to Pitlochry, second class return	7	4	
	Biscuit at Killiecrankie		2	
	Coffee and steak after arriving in Dundee		10	
	Sweeties		3	
	Two railway tickets to Broughty Ferry		7	
	For cab from thence to Kellas	1	9	
25	Church door collection		1	
26	Board and lodging	6	3	
28	Boots repairing	2		
	Dulse			½
29	Admittance to Sanger's Circus		6	
		2	17	1½

Date		Item	s.	d.
Jul	1	*People's Journal*		1
		Board and lodging	5	7
	2	Church door collection		1½
	4	Postage stamps		6
		Sunday Magazine		6
	6	Dulse		½
	7	Sweeties		3
	8	*People's Journal*		1
		Board and lodging	7	
		Biscuits		2
		Railway fare to Monifieth		6
		To my mother for butter, etc.	1	9
	9	Church door collection		3
	11	Sweeties		4
	12	Daily *Advertiser*		1
	13	Postage stamps		6
		Postage of a letter to my cousin in America		1
	14	Walker and Webster's *Dictionary of the English Language*	4	
	15	*People's Journal*		1
		Board and lodging	5	10
		Pleasure trip up the River Tay to Perth with Steam Tug Atlas	1	
		Coffee, ginger beer and biscuit on board		6½
		Sweeties		3
	16	Church door collection		2
	20	Daily *Advertiser*		1
	21	Bi-weekly *Advertiser*		2
	22	*People's Journal*		1
		Board and lodging	6	
		Sweeties		3
		Railway fare to Monifieth		6
	23	Church door collection		1
	24	To poor man on street		½
		Gooseberries		1
	27	Gooseberries		1
	29	*People's Journal*		1
		Board and lodging	5	9
		Trip to St Andrews with Steam Tug Atlas		1
		Biscuits, etc. on board		4

	Admittance to dungeon in castle of St Andrews			1
	Cayenne sweeties			2
30	Church door collection			1
	To my sister Clementina's children			
	at Monifieth			2
		2	5	8

Aug 2	*Sunday Magazine*, writing paper and envelopes	1	2
	Gooseberries		1
3	"		1
4	To testimonial to James Davison, late foreman turner at Lilybank		6
5	*People's Journal*		1
	Board and Lodging	5	10
	Sweeties		3
	Railway fare to Monifieth		6
6	Church door collection		½
	To my brother David's children at Panmure		2
9	To watch cleaning and new main spring	5	
	Gooseberries		1
12	*People's Journal*		1
	Board and lodging	6	4
	Sweeties		3
	Gooseberries		1
16	Black sugar		2
18	To make up extra expense on supper of some engines starting		10
19	*People's Journal*		1
	Board and lodging	6	1½
	Pound of apples		3
	Half pound of tea	1	8
	Railway fare to Monifieth		6
	To my mother for butter	1	
20	Church door collection		6
23	Hair cutting		2
	Dulse		1
25	Pound of apples		2
	Admission to four of the fair shows		6
26	People's Journal		1
	Board and lodging	6	8
27	Church door collection		3
31	Hot bath		6
	Sunday Magazine		7
	Sweeties and confectionery	1	2
	Ginger beer		4
		2 2	2

Sep 1	Board and lodging	6	2½
	Daily *Advertiser*		1
	Confectionery		1
	Carpet tacks		2
2	To my brother William's children at Carmylie		3
3	Church door collection	°	1
6	Sweeties		3
	Apples		1½
	Pie		2
	Boot laces		1½
8	Admission to flower show in Baxter Park		6
9	*People's Journal*		1
	Board and lodging	6	5
	Admission to flower show of my sisters, Ann and Isabella, and myself		9
	Sweeties	1	3
	Apples		3
	Postage stamps		6
14	Boots repairing		4
	Black sugar		2
16	*People's Journal*		1
	Board and lodging	6	4
	Railway fare to Monifieth		6
	Pound of apples		2
17	Church door collection		1
18	Fancy neck tie	1	
	Bottle of port wine for present to my brother Robert on the occasion of his marriage		3
19	Pies and ginger beer		8
22	Board and lodging	5	
	Sweeties and rock on the occasion of my brother's marriage	2	6
	Two cabs to take us to the station	3	
	Four railway tickets to Carnoustie	3	6
	Bottle of whisky and some wine for refreshment at marriage	6	6
	To fiddler at marriage	1	6
23	Two railway tickets from Carnoustie to Dundee	1	9
24	Church door collection		2½

23	*People's Journal*		1
27	Pound of apples		2
28	Small pocket spirit level	1	10
30	Board and lodging	7	9
	Sweeties		3
	Apples		2
	People's Journal		1
	Railway fare to Monifieth		6
		3 4	5

Oct 1	Church door collection		1
2	Box of pills		2
	Four small elastic rings		2
	Molesworth's *Pocket Book of Engineering*		
	Formulae	4	6
4	*Sunday Magazine*		7
	Pound of apples		2
7	*People's Journal* and pencil		1½
	Board and lodging	6	
	Two pound of apples		4
	Ticket for concert in Corn Exchange		6
8	Church door collection		1½
9	1½ dozen of the Waverley steel pens		6
11	Ticket for course of lectures got up by		
	Young Men's Christian Association	4	
13	Daily *Advertiser*		1
	Pound of apples		2
14	*People's Journal*		1
	Board and lodging	7	3
	Church door collection		1
	Woollen cravat	2	
14	Oxalic acid for taking iron marks out		
	of my clothes		6
	Pound of apples		1
	To poor woman on street		1
15	Church door collection		2
18	Pound of apples		2
21	*People's Journal*		1
	Thirty parts of *English Mechanic* with index	2	7
	Board and lodging	6	2
	Railway fare to Monifieth		6
	Pound of apples		1½
22	Church door collection		1
23	Top-coat repairing and dressing	1	
25	Admission to Corn Exchange to hear the		
	Rev Alessandro Gavazzi on 'Italy, Past,		
	Present and Future'		6
	Pound of apples		2
26	Daily *Advertiser*		1
28	*People's Journal*		1

	Board and lodging	6	6
	Sunday Magazine		7
	Pies and ginger beer	1	
	Two pounds of apples		3½
	To poor man on street		½
	Sweeties		3
29	Church door collection		2½
31	Pound of apples		3
		2 8	5

Nov 1	Postage stamps		6
3	Brooch repairing for my sister Ann		3
4	*People's Journal*		1
	Board and lodging	7	1
	Two bottles of lemonade		4
	Pound of apples		2½
5	Church door collection		1
	To J. Sturrock's children, Kellas		2
9	Three parts of *English Mechanic*		3
10	Bottle of quinine and box of pills		8
	Pound of apples		4
	Crackers and two small china dolls for Hallowe'en		7
11	*People's Journal*		1
	Ticket for Lilybank Foundry Soiree	1	
	Board and lodging	6	3
	Crack nuts		4
	To my mother for butter, etc.	2	4
12	Church door collection		1
	To James Sturrock's children		2
13	Pair of Wellington boots	16	6
	Pound of apples		2
	Crack nuts		3
	Sweeties		3
	To fiddler at Hallowe'en spree		10
17	Castor oil		3
	Hair oil		3
18	*People's Journal*		1
	Board and lodging	6	6
	Pound of apples		2
	Sweeties		3
	Railway ticket to Monifieth		6
	To my sister's children there		2
19	Church door collection		2½
20	Railway fare to Blairgowrie	1	10
	Admission to lecture in Town Hall of Blairgowrie		3
21	Writing paper, pen and envelopes		6
	Pair of boot laces		1
22	Ale and porter		6

	Daily *Advertiser*		I
23	Railway fare to Coupar Angus		4½
	To little girl in Coupar Angus		2
	Porter and ginger beer		5
24	Daily *Advertiser*		I
25	*People's Journal*		I
	Board and lodging	7	6
	Pair of laces		I
	Sweeties		3
27	*Advertiser*		I
28	Porter, bread and cheese		6½
29	*Advertiser*		I
30	Pound of apples		3
		3 0	4

Dec	Description		
1	*Advertiser*		1
2	*People's Journal* and *Advertiser*		2
	Board and lodging	8	9
	Railway fare to Dundee and back to Blairgowrie	2	6
	Board and lodging in Dundee	5	
	Railway fare to Monifieth		6
4	Two parts of *English Mechanic*		2
5	*Advertiser*		1
	Admission to reading in Town Hall		1
7	*Advertiser*		1
	Carriage of books from Dundee		6
8	Hair cutting		2
	New bonnet	2	
9	*Advertiser* and *People's Journal*		2
	Board and lodging	8	
	Sweeties		3
10	Church door collection		2
12	*Advertiser*		1
14	*Advertiser*		1
15	Ale and ginger beer		10
16	*People's Journal*		1
	Board and lodging	10	2
	Railway fare to Dundee and back	2	6
	Lodgings in Dundee	4	
	Half dozen of my cartes de visite	3	
	Pair of boots soling	3	6
	New elastics and repairs for do	3	
	To poor woman in street		1
	Postage stamps		6
17	Church door collection		4
19	Daily *Advertiser*		1
	Admission to lecture in Town Hall		3
21	*Advertiser*		1
23	*Advertiser* and *Journal*		2
	Board and lodging	8	11½
	Sweeties		3
24	Church door collection		1
26	*Advertiser*		1

	Admission to Mr Henry Nicoll's reading in Town Hall			6
28	Daily *Advertiser*			1
	Two pints of porter			6
30	*Advertiser* and *Journal*			2
	Board and lodging		9	9
	Railway fare to Dundee		1	10
	Two glasses of wine			8
	Board and lodging in Dundee		5	3
	Railway fare to Monifieth			6
	To my mother for washing, etc,	1	2	
31	Church door collection			1
		5	8	1½
	Total amount of expenditure – 1865	38	0	10
	Put into bank	11		
	Money in hand – 1 Jan 1866	2	8	4½
		51	9	2½

INDEX